69   This

The Start-Up Survival Guide

PEARSON
Prentice Hall
BUSINESS

Books that make you better

Books that make you better – that make you *be* better, *do* better, *feel* better. Whether you want to upgrade your personal skills or change your job, whether you want to improve your managerial style, become a more powerful communicator, or be stimulated and inspired as you work.

Prentice Hall Business is leading the field with a new breed of skills, careers and development books. Books that are a cut above the mainstream – in topic, content and delivery – with an edge and verve that will make you better, with less effort.

Books that are as sharp and smart as you are.

Prentice Hall Business.
We work harder – so you don't have to.

For more details on products, and to contact us, visit
www.pearsoned.co.uk

CHRIS J. LILLY

The Start-Up Survival Guide

What you need to know to make it through the first three years

PEARSON
Prentice Hall
BUSINESS

Harlow, England • London • New York • Boston • San Francisco • Toronto • Sydney • Tokyo • Singapore • Hong Kong
Seoul • Taipei • New Delhi • Cape Town • Madrid • Mexico City • Amsterdam • Munich • Paris • Milan

PEARSON EDUCATION LIMITED

Edinburgh Gate
Harlow CM20 2JE
Tel: +44 (0)1279 623623
Fax: +44 (0)1279 431059
Website: www.pearsoned.co.uk

First published in Great Britain in 2006

ISBN-13: 978-0-273-70832-2
ISBN-10: 0-273-70832-5

British Library Cataloguing in Publication Data
A catalogue record for this book is available from the British Library

Library of Congress Cataloging-in-Publication Data
Lilly, Chris J.
   The start-up survival guide : what you need to know to make it through the first three years / Chris J. Lilly.
      p. cm.
   Includes index.
   ISBN-13: 978-0-273-70832-2
   ISBN-10: 0-273-70832-5
   1. New business enterprises—Management—Handbooks, manuals, etc.
   2. Small business—Management—Handbooks, manuals, etc. I. Title.

   HD62.5.L55 2006
   658.1'1—dc22

                                                          2006048253
10 9 8 7 6 5 4 3 2 1
10 09 08 07 06

Cartoon illustrations by Bill Piggins

Typeset in 9.5/14.5pt Iowan Old Style by 70
Printed and bound in Great Britain by Bell & Bain Ltd

The publisher's policy is to use paper manufactured from sustainable forests.

The information contained herein is of a general nature and cannot address the particular circumstances of any particular individual or business, and it is possible that this book may contain information which becomes out of date. It is strongly recommended that you check the latest situation, especially anything relating to finance, taxation, and employment law in particular, with professional advisors before proceeding. No one should act upon the information herein without appropriate professional advice following a thorough examination of the particular situation. For professional advice, useful contacts can be found in the references given in Appendix 5.

Acknowledgements

The author acknowledges the help and data provided by many sources, but of particular note are Companies House, The Small Business Service of the UK Department of Trade and Industry, the UK Government Insolvency Service, the Institute of Directors, Business Link, R3 – the Association of Business Recovery Professionals, HM Revenue and Customs, *The Sunday Times*, Best Companies Ltd, Startup co., and Professor Robert Cressy of Cass Business School.

Thanks must also go to Rachael Stock, my editor, whose guidance has been much appreciated, as has the help from all the team at Pearson Education.

"Starting a business is like climbing a mountain"

Contents

THE BIG TOP TEN
SURVIVAL TIPS

1 Any idea for a business is only any good if there are customers who want to buy your product or service now (or in the near future). Without this you do not have a viable business proposition. It sounds obvious, but be very sure there is a big enough market.

2 Only start if you are totally convinced of the financial viability of your product/service and are prepared to commit yourself totally to making it a success.

3 Only enter a market where you, and/or your top team, have some experience and knowledge of the key market issues, e.g. how to obtain customers, pricing strategy, typical costs, etc.

4 Always watch the cash, always have a contingency fund, always plan ahead and know how you could raise additional funds quickly if necessary.

5 Never forget your customers – continually check to ensure your product/service meets, if not surpasses, customer requirements, and is differentiated from the competition. Ask yourself every day: who are the customers, what do they want, and why might they buy from me? Never be over-reliant on a single customer or supplier.

6 Consider using a mentor, or appointing one or more non-executive directors, who can provide impartial advice together with industry knowledge and contacts.

7 Plan for delays, e.g. in supplies, customer orders, recruiting staff, obtaining a loan, etc., by incorporating a contingency.

8 If you plan to grow rapidly get the right team together as soon as appropriate. Note also that the top team will change with time, so do not assume any senior position is necessarily a job for life, especially if you are using other people's money!

9 Seek professional advice (i.e. legal, financial, etc.) whenever necessary and appropriate.

10 When preparing your business plan recognize that entrepreneurs tend to be overly optimistic – so ensure your figures are realistic, and incorporate a sensitivity analysis.

Introduction

It's a daunting fact for all those starting a business that, on average, more than one in three of start-up businesses don't survive the first three years! The message is clear: to be successful, first you need to survive. Without losing sight of those big dreams what you really need to know in the early years is *why so many businesses fail early on* and *what you must understand and do to have the best chance of being in the 66% that survive the first three years (rather than the 33% that fail)*. This book provides as much as possible of the information and advice that young growing companies need in those first years. In particular it highlights the pitfalls to be avoided at all costs, so that at least you are prepared and in a better position to eventually be successful and in business for the long term. *The Start-Up Survival Guide* looks at being successful from the viewpoint of what can so easily go wrong – and how to avoid those situations.

All managers running businesses need to be aware of the statistics, which unfortunately show that although many people are entrepreneurial and there are many businesses started annually, according to the UK Department of Trade & Industry Small Business Service some 10% of those fail within a year, 25% within 2 years and some 33% within 3 years!

The purpose of this book is to help prospective and existing entrepreneurs become aware of why companies so often go under and, more importantly, what you can do to prevent such failures. If any company can survive as a result of its founders or managers having read this *Survival Guide*, then it will have proved its worth. In the following pages the reasons for businesses failing are analyzed: if you follow the contents you should be in a much better position to weather the storms encountered in growing a business.

Unbelievable as it might sound, the road to failure for start-ups may well start at the very conception of the business! Why do I say this? Because there are a number of essential ingredients required for a successful business, and most of these have to be addressed ideally even before it gets going. These ingredients include:

▶ having a differentiated product or service

▶ identifying a customer base that will want to buy your product/service, in the right timescales, at the price you propose selling at, and which is willing to buy from you

▶ the boss and top team ideally having appropriate management experience with a background in the sector or, as a minimum, having some knowledge about the whole plethora of issues which businesses have to address

▶ ensuring an adequate cashflow at all times. Almost nine out of ten companies fail because they either directly or indirectly run out of cash. There are of course numerous reasons why this happens including:
  – inadequate sales
  – sales price too high
  – competition with better product/service
  – high production costs, including poor productivity
  – inadequate management
  – market disappears
  – *force majeure* (circumstances beyond one's control)
  – inadequate insurance (following a disaster/mishap)
  – interest rates increasing so debt becomes unaffordable
  – foreign exchange rates go against the company making products too expensive to sell abroad.

All of these ingredients are addressed in much more detail in the relevant sections of this book.

Who is the book for?

This book is for all budding entrepreneurs, and all those already involved in running a small business. Whether you are thinking of creating your own start-up, are part of a university or corporate spin-out, are buying into a company, are being promoted or are already in a director's role where you have responsibility for the company's success, this *Survival Guide* is for you. It looks at starting and growing a business from a different perspective to most other handbooks of this type. Most focus on how you might be successful. In the real world, the challenge in the first three years is all about surviving; being successful is the icing on the cake and, for most, usually comes later on! Here we address the basics to ensure not only that you survive, but also stand a chance of eventually being really successful.

The text is written around the business environment in the United Kingdom and hence makes reference to the relevant UK laws and taxation where applicable. However much of the book can still be of benefit to any entrepreneur or business manager wherever they are based.

Getting the most from this book

When you're starting a business you have many demands on your time. This *Survival Guide* is therefore designed to be dipped into as and when you can or need some immediate help, as an alternative to reading right through from cover to cover.

For a quick fix and a reminder of key start-up business issues, go straight to Chapter 1, Crash course in survival. To help those of you who are 'time restricted' the chapters have been split into easily read bites, and at the end of each section or chapter is a list of *Top Tips* to help you on the road to success in your business.

For those who are already encountering issues or problems, there are *Emergency Packs* at the beginning of many of the key chapters, which highlight various warning signs and suggested fixes to rectify possible disaster scenarios.

Whatever your situation, I hope this book gives you the vital insights that will help you through the survival phase, and then on to very great success. Good luck!

1

Crash course in survival
a quick-read chapter for quick survival

In a rush? Here's the quick guide to the vital principles of business, flagging the key issues you need to be aware of. Subsequent chapters then cover these issues in the kind of detail you really need to make sure you've got your survival strategy in place. As a start we have the 5 Cs for success, shown in Table 1.1.

Table 1.1   The 5 Cs for success

5 Cs for success	
a simple *aide-memoire* for a successful business	
1 Cash	ensure you have plenty to pay the bills
2 Customers	keep them 'delighted' with good products, meeting their evolving requirements
3 Competitors	be aware of them and what they offer, and ensure you are able to differentiate yourself from them
4 'Can do' culture	almost everything is possible with the right 'can do' culture
5 Communications	maintain good communications with all parties, i.e. customers, suppliers, investors, your bank and, not least, your staff

THE 5 Cs

Cash

Cash is essential to get started. It is essential to remain in business. Lack of it means the demise of the business.

"No cash – no company"

Entrepreneurs are always over-optimistic, so as a rule of thumb you would be wise to consider the implications of assuming an extra 50% for costs, reducing your revenue forecasts by 50%, or extending the timescale for specific revenue achievement by 50%. Doing this will indicate whether your business plan is truly viable.

Customers

Without them you will have no revenues! Ensure when you start that you know who your customers are likely to be, that they have expressed an interest in your product/service, will actually buy from you, and are prepared to pay your envisaged selling price.

"No customers – no company"

Competition

If you are lucky there may not be any competition initially, but don't count on that situation lasting for long because others will soon enter your market if they see you being successful. Learn from your competitors whenever possible; ensure you are doing all the good things that they are doing. Furthermore, ensure your offering is better than theirs by having a unique feature perhaps, or some form of major differentiation which will attract your prospective customers to your products/services.

'Can do' culture

Recruit people you know are a good cultural fit, you know can do the job and who won't let you down. The company culture will then follow automatically without you even having to necessarily define it.

A good positive company culture usually leads to a productive and successful company.

Communications

You would not believe how many problems are created within businesses as a result of poor (or no) communication. Suffice to say the best and most successful organizations are those which communicate to all levels of staff. For instance, in such companies, the lowest ranks are usually just as aware of the company's mission, its products, etc., as senior staff.

When management communicates with its workers there is less chance of misunderstandings, a sense of cohesion and belonging is created, and morale is generally improved by the mere fact that senior executives are taking time out to communicate with them about what is going on.

Communication should always be a two-way mechanism and any communication events, be they a simple monthly meeting, or an annual sales conference or whatever, are a chance for management to obtain the views of staff at all levels. It is not uncommon for staff lower down in the company to actually have a better idea of what is actually going on within a company, and its problems, than more senior managers.

MONEY

Money (cash) is so fundamental to the success of a business that I feel that it is important to reiterate the message. Most businesses fail, either directly or indirectly, due to having insufficient cash and no other reason. Hence the well-known expression:

❝*Cash is king*❞

If you have sufficient cash in the bank to pay your existing and future bills, and a steady continuing flow of cash from sales, then in all probability your business can survive.

Businesses can decide to cease trading for a number of reasons apart from not being financially viable, for instance, owners retiring, partners not being able to agree on matters such as strategy, or on operational matters etc. However in this section we focus on the subject of cash – how cash is generated and how it disappears.

Cash generation

Cash is generated by the provision of a product or service. The amount charged for the product or service and the quantity sold determine the total cash revenue income.

The pricing for the product or service can be on a 'bottom-up' basis, i.e. cost plus, where the costs are determined and a mark-up applied to arrive at the selling price. Mark-ups can vary tremendously depending on the product or service, and whether you are a manufacturer, retailer or whatever, but can be anything in the range of 10 to 100%. As a new business you need to understand the pricing strategies of your competitors to know what sort of mark-up might be applicable in your industry, which is why industry experience is so important.

The other pricing strategy is 'top-down', whereby the pricing is assessed based on what the market will stand, i.e. market pricing. Once again it is vital to know the going rate for your type of product or service in order to be able to make realistic pricing assessments.

There is also some science to pricing, which takes into account concepts such as elasticity of demand, which factors in that:

▶ you cannot increase your prices with impunity – sales volume will start to fall at some pricing point

▶ decreasing your price should, all things being equal, increase your sales volume, but this does have an increasingly adverse impact on your profit margin.

Even good news can be a problem in that increasing sales may mean extra overhead costs, for instance having to purchase an extra piece of machinery, which might decrease your profitability for a while until your increased sales are sufficient to make operation of the additional machine fully viable. The bottom line is that there is, more often than not, an optimal price for a product or service. (For more on this, read *Smarter Pricing* by Tony Cram – see Appendix 5.)

Market knowledge and experience help considerably on the subject of pricing, which is why banks, venture capitalists and business angels usually only like to invest in people with at least some experience of the market in question.

Businesses in their start-up phase will not generally have sufficient sales revenues in the initial period to outweigh their costs, and hence external funding is often required. Ideally such a funding gap is best plugged by you, the business owner, from your own resources; this is because you are not then beholden to others, or in a position where you have to give up a stake in your company. Some people can find the necessary funding from raiding their savings, cashing in an endowment mortgage, extending the mortgage on their house or using a redundancy payout. If this does not raise sufficient funds, or none of these options is practicable for whatever reason, the next step is to tap family and friends, although recognize that you may not be popular if they don't get their money back! This is a very delicate area which should be given a lot of thought.

After these sources you might go to a bank for a loan, which for a small amount of maybe up to £20,000 might be unsecured, but anything larger is likely to have to be on a secured basis, for instance your house might have to be offered as security, or alternatively the bank will ask for someone to guarantee the loan, so that in the event that you default, the bank still gets its money. Bear in mind however that the guarantor stands a one in three chance of losing their money – based on the statistics – so they need to be able to afford to stand any loss.

Banks are also the place to go for an overdraft. However, overdrafts should be used with care and ideally only as an aid to cashflow, for instance for paying suppliers pending payment of sales invoices, etc. In the normal course of events overdrafts should not be used for capital expenditure, for which a long-term loan is generally a better solution.

For young entrepreneurs under 30 requiring less than £5,000 to create a start-up, a loan from The Prince's Trust might be worth considering (see website reference in Appendix 5).

In some cases grants of various sorts can be made available and there are specialist websites which provide all the requisite information (see Appendix 5).

The next source of plugging the funding gap in the early days is to use 'other people's money', namely that of business angels, if the amount required is up to around £500,000. Typically, individual business angels are prepared to fund anything from £10,000 to £50,000, with some prepared to go as high as £250,000. It can happen that a small number will club together to raise a larger combined amount. Business angels will of course want a stake in your business, which might be anything up to 50% or even higher, and they may be passive or may wish to take an active part in the running of the business – which can sometimes be of immense value in itself if they have the right background and experience.

For larger amounts you need to consider venture capital. Chapter 16 considers the issues around raising venture capital in more detail. In brief, most venture capitalists (VCs) like to invest in excess of £1M and some will not consider less than £5M. Like business angels, VCs will want a stake in your business in return for their investment, hence your stake is reduced.

The stake in your business which a VC or business angel might require will depend on their assessment of the market value of your company, the amount of money you are looking to raise and the amount they are prepared to invest. Typically VCs will look for anything up to 45% (although sometimes more), and many are reluctant to have a stake of much less than 30% at start-up.

Cash out

It is all so easy to spend money as we all know. In business it is important to spend only the right/sensible amounts and at the right time. Moreover, the expenditure should have been pre-planned so that you know in advance what you have to spend money on and when. This is called a budget forecast. You can then compare your actual monthly expenditure with your budgeted figure, and if there is a significant variance you should understand why it has come about. Experience helps considerably in preparing an accurate budget, in respect of remembering to include all foreseen costs, having a good handle on the magnitude of those costs, and allowing a reasonable contingency for any underestimating of costs, as well as for the cost of any items which you might have forgotten.

There are numerous reasons why expenditure might exceed your budget including:

- incorrect figures in budget
- forgetting to budget for something
- price increases not allowed for
- bills arriving at different times to those forecast
- having to pay staff more than anticipated
- poor credit management.

Once again some knowledge and experience of your industry helps significantly in achieving as accurate a budget forecast as possible and is another reason why banks, venture capitalists and business angels usually only like to invest in people with at least some experience of the market in question.

PEOPLE – GETTING THE RIGHT STAFF AT THE RIGHT TIME

Some businesses start off as a sole trader business and never grow beyond this size; others start this way but grow over time; and yet others start with the intention of growing quickly and recruiting a team of people almost immediately, and then grow rapidly from this base.

As a business founder, whether a sole trader or one of a management team, if your business is to both grow and succeed you must understand, amongst other things:

▶ the marketplace

▶ the potential customers

▶ the potential suppliers

▶ pricing strategy, e.g. margins, mark-up rates, etc.

▶ production (where relevant) and overhead costs.

If you are a sole trader you need all this knowledge yourself. If you are a company with staff you need people with this specific knowledge, with a background in fields such as sales and marketing, operations/production, finance, product development, etc., as appropriate. This expertise should help you win sales and grow your business. It is a fact that many businesses do not grow simply because either the boss is not prepared to relinquish responsibility by recruiting additional staff, or because the financial investment in people is never made.

Interestingly there are some instances where a company ceases to trade not because of any cash issue, but because, for instance:

▶ it realizes that it does not have the either the right people to do the job, or cannot find or afford to recruit them

▶ the start-up team found that they just could not get on together, and decide to call it a day.

Apart from recruiting people to win new business and to supply the product or service there is another area which should never be overlooked, and that is the accounts department. Given the importance of financial controls in running any sort of business, as you grow to become a business with significant cash flows, one of the best people investments you could make is to employ an accounts clerk. Of course, if your business is small, it means you either have to be your own accounts clerk, or you can outsource this task to a specialist. If a larger business, then you should employ someone to act in this role as soon as possible. If you have pretensions of grandeur and plan to be a multimillion pound company within a year, you should also consider appointing a financial director (FD) early on. Indeed if you are raising funds from a VC they may well insist on an FD being appointed within maybe six months of you starting up.

If you get the foundations of your business right by recruiting a good team of people at the start, then you are so much more likely to grow in accordance with your plans and become a long-term success story.

NEGOTIATION

This might appear to be a strange heading for a crash survival guide. However, if you think about it, business is all about negotiation. You buy products and services from your suppliers, and you sell products or services to your customers. Each of these purchasing or selling activities requires negotiation skills; for instance, you should be negotiating the very best deals on whatever you buy, and you can expect that your customers are likely to negotiate with you on whatever you are selling. Such negotiations are not always about money either; they can include a myriad of things such as delivery dates, product specifications, quality, commercial terms and conditions, etc.

So if you do not already have any negotiating skills then you would be well advised to learn them, or hone them if you already have some experience, as soon as you possibly can. Experience shows that really successful business people are invariably good negotiators!

Surprisingly to some, there is a considerable amount of skill in effective negotiating, and some prior thought before negotiation starts will prove invaluable. Key negotiating tactics include:

1 Work out what your ideal outcome might be.

2 Work out, as best you can, what the other party's ideal outcome might be. Determine, in particular, whether the other party has any particular desires or requirements apart from simply money (or whatever).

3 Work out the worst acceptable terms which you could accept. When considering the terms bear in mind all the elements of a deal, not just price. For instance, maybe the other party just wants to shift goods quickly irrespective of price (because they have to pay their VAT bill perhaps).

4 Do not rush into the deal or try to complete the deal quickly – some of the best negotiators are extremely patient.

5 During the negotiation watch the body language of the other party – you can learn a lot from a sigh, scratching of the head, etc.

6 Try to formulate the deal in such a way that the other party benefits from features which they regard as being important, but which you can provide at little or no cost or effort.

7 Show respect and build rapport wherever possible. You may wish to buy or sell from the other party again, and developing a relationship where there is respect between the parties is likely to prove of immense long-term benefit.

8 Do not forget that there may be some restrictions on what the other party can offer/agree to, so it is important for you to determine what these are early on in the negotiations – but do not ask bluntly, ask in a circumspect manner. This way you can work out how far you can negotiate.

9 Keep the negotiations businesslike and do not let emotion cloud your judgement.

10 Remember to 'close' the deal by agreeing all the different aspects of the negotiation, for instance the money issues, delivery, quality, etc. (which you should have identified prior to the negotiation). Summarize any agreement to ensure clarity and full understanding on both sides before departing.

PLAN FOR DELAYS

It seems to be one of those immutable laws of life that, despite your best endeavours, delays of various sorts are almost inevitable. It is therefore prudent to:

1 Not be optimistic in your planning, since this will only make matters worse.

2 Incorporate a contingency element in your planning which can be used to mitigate any delays.

3 Ensure activities are adequately resourced, especially if timing is an important issue, and allow for resource difficulties, e.g. staff sickness, delays in funding/financing, etc.

MANAGEMENT OF PROBLEMS

Management denial is the biggest problem!

You cannot bury your head in the sand if there are problems. It is very tempting to do so, but if you speak to anyone whose business has failed as a result of being in denial, their advice (with the benefit of hindsight) is always to face up to problems and take remedial action at the earliest oppor- tunity – while you still have a chance of correcting things.

Early action is important

Once you are on the slippery slope the downhill momentum develops very fast. Once the alarm bells start to ring you cannot ignore them and hope they will go away – they never do. By far the best course of action is to face up to the issues while you have some chance of fixing things. Leave them and it will be too late. All your hard work and that of your loyal employees will have been to no avail.

Need for early warning signals

Obtaining those early warning signals is essential. It is for this reason that you are advised to have a regular review of key business performance parameters. Every business, big or small, should have a regular review of its performance, and in bigger companies monthly board meetings are an ideal time to review performance. Even sole proprietors should take time out from the day-to-day running of their business to review their progress at least monthly.

Get feedback from customers

No customers – no business! It is therefore absolutely essential that you not only attract new customers (in order to grow) but, just as importantly, you ensure that your existing customers stay with you. It is therefore wise to always keep in touch with your customers and:

▶ obtain customer feedback regularly, so that any problems do not come as a surprise

▶ questionnaires are a tempting way of obtaining feedback, but people are only prepared to fill them in at most once a year (if that). So you also need to develop other techniques for obtaining critical feedback. Anyone who has face-to-face contact with a customer is in a good position to obtain feedback. The key is to make sure every opportunity for such comment is taken, that it is collated and fed back to someone who can do something about it, and that any necessary action is indeed put in place. A business lunch can often be a good way of finding out some home truths, especially over the brandy!

▶ review key performance parameters monthly.

Monthly management monitoring

It is essential for every business, be it a start-up or a well-established company, to review key business performance parameters monthly, and sometimes in dire circumstances even more frequently, e.g. weekly. Some typical parameters which you might consider reviewing are given on page 59.

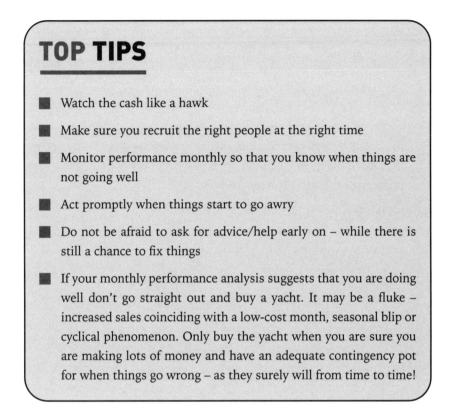

TOP **TIPS**

- Watch the cash like a hawk

- Make sure you recruit the right people at the right time

- Monitor performance monthly so that you know when things are not going well

- Act promptly when things start to go awry

- Do not be afraid to ask for advice/help early on – while there is still a chance to fix things

- If your monthly performance analysis suggests that you are doing well don't go straight out and buy a yacht. It may be a fluke – increased sales coinciding with a low-cost month, seasonal blip or cyclical phenomenon. Only buy the yacht when you are sure you are making lots of money and have an adequate contingency pot for when things go wrong – as they surely will from time to time!

PART ONE

The vital stuff

2

Getting started

so as to survive in the long term

ARE YOU UP TO BEING AN ENTREPRENEUR?

What's this all about?

It means that not everyone is cut out to be an entrepreneur, or top boss, and it is therefore helpful to have a little introspection before you really get started to determine whether you really have what it takes to be successful, either as a sole trader, or as one of the top team in a multimillion pound business.

Most companies start off with just one employee – you. You may stay as the only employee or proprietor for ever, or your business may grow over time. With just you to run things you need to recognize that you will have to perform all the functions of a big business, including sales and marketing, production/provision of service, delivery driver, finance director, accounts clerk, etc. You will appreciate that there can be a great deal of responsibility with no one to share the load. It is not surprising therefore that many sole traders become tense at times.

Unfortunately the worries do not go away in a larger business because, although you might have other people to share your worries, people problems can just add to the burden, money problems are just that much bigger, and you have the responsibility of paying staff at the end of each week or month, together with tax, VAT, and suppliers every so often.

So, what are the qualities required of a successful entrepreneur or businessperson? The list is probably endless, but some of the more important qualities include:

- ▶ tenacity
- ▶ commitment
- ▶ conviction
- ▶ sense of humour
- ▶ ability to get on well with people
- ▶ basic numeracy skills (to handle the money)
- ▶ selling skills
- ▶ negotiating skills
- ▶ planning skills
- ▶ ability to delegate once you have staff.

If you do not have any of these qualities, you should try to acquire them, or alternatively recruit people who do have them. Hopefully you are now adequately confident in your abilities that you are prepared to proceed and give the business everything you've got!

The Business Link website (see Appendix 5) has a personal development planner which helps you understand your current management skill capabilities, and then provides an action plan which should help you develop any weaker areas which might warrant some attention (see www.businesslink.gov.uk/pdp).

BACKGROUND TO SUCCESS

It can be interesting, and potentially very useful to know – as a new entrepreneur – how successful businesspeople have become so. For instance, do certain business sectors offer a greater chance of success, is there a geographical region where you may be more likely to succeed, do your genes make a difference, and does education make a difference?

Of course there are different measures of success; some people will be more than happy to have established a business that interests them and provides them with an acceptable income. Others may wish to become a millionaire before they would regard themselves as being successful. It is noteworthy that the 300 richest people in the UK, each of whom has assets in excess of £100M, have been successful in a broad range of business sectors, as shown in Table 2.1

Table 2.1 Analysis of successful entrepreneurs by industry

Sector	Percentage of people in each sector
Property	15%
Retail (non-food)	13%
Industry	12%
Finance	11%
Landed gentry	10%
Technology	8%
Media/publishing/entertainment	8%
Hotels/restaurants/holidays	5%
Food/drink	5%
Transport	3%
Pop stars	3%
Other	7%

[Source: Data derived from *The Sunday Times* Rich List]

In summary some 50% of these successful businesspeople operated in one of just four sectors, namely property, retail (non food), industry and finance.

If you think your parents' trade or profession might have an impact on your entrepreneurial success, it would appear that this is not the case at all – since the top 300 success stories mentioned above have parents from right across the spectrum, from professionals to manual labourers. On the question of education, interestingly, there is a surprisingly high proportion of successful entrepreneurs who either did *not* go into, or complete, full-time further education.

It follows that money can be made in virtually any business sector, that your parents' jobs do not have much impact on your potential to succeed (although them lending you some money might!), and further education would not appear to be a prerequisite for success.

PRODUCT/SERVICE

It is all very well deciding that you want to run your own business, but you must have a clear idea about the product or service you wish to offer. Not only this, you must be able to assess the size of the market, and the competition, so as to be able to determine how much business might come your way.

You must be absolutely sure that there are customers out there who want your product or service, will pay the price you are considering, and who are actually prepared to buy from you – as opposed to any competition. So many people just start up without considering these basic business elements, and are surprised when they have to close down within a short period of starting through lack of customers.

FUNDING

Most businesses need money in order to get going. In the simplest example such funding might be required just to fund the gap between buying your products and selling them. If providing a service it may be just to keep you going – before getting your first piece of business. More complicated businesses, for instance a manufacturing or high-tech company, will need funding to pay for machinery, research and development, etc.

The amount of funding needed by any business will vary enormously from maybe as little as a few hundred pounds to over £1M.

If you can fund the business from your own resources then this is definitely the best way to proceed, for example many businesses have been started following redundancy payments and others have been started using extended mortgages. If you fund the business yourself it means you do not need to go cap in hand to anybody else, there is no question of reducing your stake in your business, and you do not need to answer difficult questions about your business plan.

As soon as you have to ask someone else for money then things start to get a little more complicated. If you do decide you do not have sufficient funds yourself then the next obvious ports of call are friends and relatives who may give you a loan, although they may insist on a stake in the business.

If this does not work you might consider various start-up grants and/or loans, and there are some very good websites that list all the various grant offerings (see Appendix 5). More detail about all the different funding sources is given on page 70, and Chapter 16 provides more detailed information relating to venture capital.

PEOPLE

If you are not planning to stay as a solo operation then your business will need partners, or managers and staff. The importance of getting the right people recruited at the right time cannot be overemphasized and is a key principle stressed throughout this book. A good senior management team, irrespective of whether it is established at the outset or is built up over time as the company grows, is crucial. There is little doubt that if you can recruit people from your network of contacts, whom you know can do the job, are a good cultural fit, and you can afford to hire them, then do so, since experience indicates that this is potentially the smartest way to get off to a quick start and to grow. The same philosophy also applies to other staff.

However, irrespective of the level of staff, do avoid hiring people just because you are good friends socially, or you owe them a favour or whatever; unless you are sure they can do the job well and will be a good cultural fit, do not be tempted to employ them.

Remember also, in these days of extensive employment legislation, it is very difficult to terminate an employee's contract once they have been hired, especially if they have been with you for some time. Putting the wrong people in place can spell disaster for small companies, and can also be problematic for larger ones, so it is advisable to do your best to recruit the right people first time around.

ACCOMMODATION

Many businesses are operated from home, and in these cases accommodation is not generally a major problem unless, that is, you are on the telephone trying to sound like a professional company when the dog barks or the baby cries, quickly dispelling any such illusion.

Although there is a trend towards working from home, even in larger companies, the vast majority of businesses employing staff need some form of accommodation to house them, such as an office, industrial unit or whatever.

Why is this being mentioned as an issue in surviving for the long term? The answer is simply that, except for those businesses which can operate in short-lease accommodation or serviced offices, most businesses have to enter into a long lease in order to occupy the property. This in itself is not a problem; the problem is that most landlords like to lock-in their tenants for a long time, and hence lease durations of ten years are not unusual, albeit sometimes with break clauses at an intermediate time, e.g. five years. Thus, as soon as you sign a lease, you are committed to the rent payments for the duration of the term, and if your business takes a turn for the worse and you find the need to downsize, you may have a problem. Having said this, it is often possible, and indeed quite common, to sublet the premises (with the agreement of the landlord). However if your sub-tenant lets you down by not paying the rent, you may be stuck with the rent commitments. Sometimes, if the landlord is reasonable, it is possible to transfer the lease to the new tenant, clearly the most desirable option, but this is by no means guaranteed.

So what is the message? It is to only enter a lease agreement with your eyes wide open, fully understanding the implications should the business either take a downturn or alternatively (looking on the brighter side), require larger premises earlier than anticipated. Legal advice is always advised to help you fully understand the implications of any lease/tenancy agreement.

TOP **TIPS**

■ Don't worry about the sector which is likely to make you the most successful – go for the sector that you know something about and/or think you will be happiest working in

■ Don't worry about your background – people from all types of backgrounds can be successful, even those without further education

■ The secret to success is tenacity, commitment, vision, and a lot of luck

■ Ensure there is customer demand for your product/service

■ Recruit people you are completely confident can do the job

■ Understand fully the commitment that leasing accommodation means before signing anything

3

Business plans and planning

Business plans are an essential part of business and every start-up should have one. Indeed it is often not until you come to write the business plan that you realize the myriad issues which have to be considered and addressed before you can even get started.

Even existing businesses will need a business plan whenever they need to raise outside funding. It is also good practice to update your business plan at least once a year, so that you have a record of where you are going, and what you are trying to do, for the benefit of the senior management team and ultimately, for the benefit of all stakeholders, i.e. staff, customers, shareholders, and suppliers.

There is no hard and fast format for business plans; as long as all the relevant information is contained in the document that is usually sufficient. A plan that is too long, say in excess of 40 pages (excluding appendices) is also indicative of poorly focused management thinking.

Unfortunately business plans only represent the management's vision and hopes as at the date of writing. While the document on a particular day may be excellent and an accurate reflection of the proposed (or existing) business, things usually have a habit of changing, such that, for instance in a year's time, the sales projections might turn out to have been grossly overestimated – because a new competitor entered the market, or because a freak storm impacted sales, for example. Clearly there are numerous reasons why a business plan and its integral financial forecasts may not turn out to be accurate.

It is also important to identify as many risks as possible and to quantify the implications of these risks in the financial statements.

A typical business plan will have the headings shown in Table 3.1.

Table 3.1   Business plan chapters

1	Index
2	Executive summary
3	Product/service
	What it is
	Technology
	Demonstrator available
	Technical viability
	Differentiators
	Intellectual property/patents/copyright
	SWOT
4	Market
	Size
	Geography
	Market share
	Growth rates
	Competition
	Barriers to entry
5	Customers and sales strategy
	Who are they?
	List real names
	Customer statements of desire to buy
	Do they want to buy the product?
	When will they buy it?
	How much will they pay?
	How much will they buy?
	Will they buy from this company?

Table 3.1 continued

	Will they insist on competitive procurement?
	Will they share their order requirements around?
	Will they reveal all the above information to a third party doing due diligence
	Sales team and strategy
6	Company structure and operations (make two chapters if necessary)
	Business model
	Company structure
	Competitive edge
	Operational arrangements
	R&D plans
	Manufacturing plans
	Service arrangements
	Timescales/programme
7	Management
	Team (careers to date and relevant experience)
	CEO with relevant experience/competence/focus/integrity/credibility
	Director shareholdings
8	Financial
	Financial projections
	Margins
	Revenue growth
	Capex levels
	Profitability
9	Risks
	Technical
	Commercial
	Financial
	Other
10	Prospects for investor exit/exit potential
	Timescale
	Potential financial gain on exit (IRR > x 3 money invested)
11	Conclusions
12	Contact data for more information

Writing a business plan is not particularly easy, even for experienced hands. Hopefully the headings in Table 3.1 above, together with the subheadings will provide sufficient pointers as to the content. Subsequent chapters will provide further ideas as to content within each heading. Appendix 5 also contains details of useful websites which give more information about starting up a business and preparing a business plan. In particular you might wish to visit the Business Link website listed under 'Getting started'.

In any business plan the financial section is one of the most important. Most things boil down to money at the end of the day, either a cost or an income. It follows therefore that the financial projections give a very good indication as to what is going on in the business and, from the base financial data, the long-term profitability becomes clear. At this stage you can see whether you have a winning business proposition or not. For those who are not so good on spreadsheets there are software programs available which greatly facilitate preparing and presenting the financial projections.

Remember that if you are looking for external funding, the potential investor(s) will require a copy of your business plan and will read it in minute detail and, invariably, if potentially interested, will have numerous questions to ask of you, which will really test your thinking and business acumen.

TOP TIPS

- Keep the total length of the business plan to less than 30 pages
- Cover additional information in appendices if you must
- If you are unable to get the message over in a one or two page executive summary you probably shouldn't even be trying to go ahead with your venture. Alternatively get someone else to see whether they can write the executive summary succinctly for you

4

Money matters

MONEY EMERGENCY PACK

If you are already experiencing money problems, Table 4.1 below lists some of the more common financial warning signs, suggests possible causes, and proposes possible solutions which might help resolve your problem.

Table 4.1   Some financial warning signs, causes and solutions

Warning signs	Possible causes	Possible solutions
Shortage of cash	No or reduced sales	Address sales and marketing issues
	Selling price too low	Re-evaluate pricing strategy
	Direct costs too high	Review direct cost base
	Overhead costs too high	Review overhead costs
	Over-expansion without adequate funding	Consider overdrafts, loans and/or additional equity input
Unsold stock increasing	Reduced sales volume	Try sales/discounts to remove old stock
	Overproduction	Determine optimal production
	Obsolete products	Sell off at discount
	Product/service not appealing to customers	Improve/update products

Table 4.1 continued

Warning signs	Possible causes	Possible solutions
No customer enquiries	Reduced visibility in the marketplace	Review sales and marketing activity: try or increase advertising
	Phones not answered	Check manning of phone lines
	Fax not working	Check fax working
	Internet shopping website down	Check website working
Overdraft increasing without corresponding increase in sales	Overdraft being used for core borrowing rather than fluctuations in working capital	Undertake complete financial review
Debtor days increasing	Inadequate focus on chasing payments due	Check processes, e.g. are bills going out on time, are there staff to chase payments, are the staff chasing when they should, are payments being recorded when they come in?
Invoices taking longer to get out	Inadequate billing processes/staffing levels	Review accounting function processes and staffing levels
Unable to pay VAT or PAYE due to lack of cash	Shortage of cash	See above
	VAT or NI cash being spent on other things	Put VAT and NI cash in escrow account
Increase in bad debts	Deterioration in marketplace	Review marketplace with sales team
	Inadequate chasing of payments due	Check processes and staffing in accounts dept
	Disputes over supply/ quality, etc.	Check if customers have problems with product
Increase in number of red invoice reminders	Non-payment in time due to:	See Shortage of cash (Warning signs)
	–Poor payments process –Inadequate staff –Lack of cash	Negotiate alternative contractual terms if possible
Overheads increasing	Poor management Expenditure on wrong things Inadequate monitoring of overhead costs	Review where increases are occurring and address

Table 4.1 continued

Warning signs	Possible causes	Possible solutions
	New product not yet achieving required sales levels	
Acquisition draining cash	Inadequate financing Poor financial planning	Either need to reduce operating costs dramatically or obtain additional finance urgently

MONEY MATTERS IN A NUTSHELL

In a nutshell:

❝no cash = no company❞

You can have an attractive profit and loss (P&L) and balance sheet, but if you have no cash in the bank (or under the bed) then you cannot pay your bills and your creditors will ultimately call in the liquidators. This is unless you have foreseen the problem, which all responsible managers should, and indeed are required to under the Companies Act, since trading while insolvent is illegal and directors can be called to account.

The basics which must be understood and followed by any business large or small include the following:

▶ establish and maintain a good book-keeping system

▶ recruit an accounts clerk as soon as one can be afforded; alternatively for small businesses you can outsource this activity. By doing this there will be no excuse for not having all the data available for monitoring the financial health of the business

▶ purchase a good accounts software package – such as Sage or TAS – it makes life easier all round, does many of the necessary calculations and generates performance parameters for you automatically

▶ monitor cash in hand at regular intervals, e.g. weekly or at least monthly

▶ when your costs exceed income calculate the rate at which you are spending cash ('cash burn') so as to determine when you will run out

▶ monitor debtor days, i.e. average length of time you are granting credit to your customers; if it exceeds your stated terms then you need to keep a close eye on those customers not paying on time, and establish an action plan to get the money owed. If you can afford it, it may pay to have an accounts person whose responsibility includes chasing customers whose payments are overdue

▶ have a reputable accountant review your finances. As and when you become large enough, and you can afford it, recruit a finance manager/director. Note that most VCs will insist on there being a finance director in place before they will inject their funding, or at least request that one be put in place within, say, six months

▶ monitor the financials at monthly board meetings. There should be a financial report, prepared and submitted by the finance director (FD), with the support of the CEO. Even if you are just a sole trader, or a very small business, you could still benefit from analyzing your financial performance on a monthly basis. Apart from a written statement of progress and issues, a monthly financial report should show the following financial data:

1 expenditure in the past month, broken down by major category

2 budgeted expenditure in the past month, broken down by major category

3 sales in the past month, broken down by category

4 budgeted sales in the past month, broken down by category

5 cumulative expenditure to date in current financial year

6 budgeted cumulative expenditure to date in current financial year

7 cumulative sales to date in current financial year

8 budgeted cumulative sales to date in current financial year

▶ monitor costs: ensure that cheques are signed by two parties (unless you are a sole trader) at least one of whom is a director

▶ establish a procedure for who may spend money

▶ ensure expenditure is authorized, and is budgeted, and in accordance with the business plan

▶ have a creditor payment policy, ideally one where you make payment just before your suppliers terms state payment will be due, thereby ensuring you establish and maintain a good credit record. A good credit record is important for when you want to open new credit accounts with suppliers, or you want a bank loan, or you are trying to sell the company for a good price

▶ introduce defined payment terms as part of your terms and conditions. 30 day payment terms are the de facto business standard, and you will be lucky to improve on this, although some businesses can insist on payment with order, or on delivery. Be aware that some larger firms try to negotiate longer payment terms such as 60 days, and some have even been known to impose 120 days!

❝No cash = no company❞

TOP TIPS

■ When cashflow is not established, i.e. before revenues are starting to really flow, determine how much cash you are spending on a monthly basis (known as 'cash burn rate'), with projections for 6 to 12 months ahead, which is monitored and reviewed at board level at least monthly

■ Even better is to have a 'days to meltdown' parameter, which measures the number of days you have left before you run out of money – given your current cash burn rate

■ Trading while not being able to pay your bills, or having a reasonable idea as to how you are going to pay those bills, is unlawful. When you reach this stage you are obliged to call in an insolvency practitioner. If you are a limited company and you fail to bring in an expert promptly then you will not benefit from the personal protection granted to you by operating as a limited company and you can personally be called to account. This is known as unlawful trading and the penalties can be very severe in the worst case

■ Consider a 'rainy day fund', or as an accountant would call it a 'contingency' pot. Especially for start-ups it is almost vital to be able to fall back on this reserve pot of gold as and when you find that your business plan forecasts are not going according to plan. Larger companies do this as a matter of routine; such contingency funds usually appear under the heading 'cash and reserves' in financial account

CASHFLOW

Cash is king – never let anyone tell you otherwise!

We have already mentioned the importance of cash – to companies both large and small. Even large multinationals have been known to close down because they just did not have enough cash to finance their operations. Cash is an even more important consideration for smaller companies, since they may not have the capacity to obtain further loans, etc., to relieve the pressure of cash shortage.

For start-ups common causes of revenues not flowing in from customers include:

▶ changed customer timescales

▶ changed customer requirements

▶ delays in producing product, e.g. R&D delays, production problems, etc.

There are a whole host of reasons why cash might not flow as forecast, but suffice to say, the best solution is to address the cashflow problem early on, ideally at a forecasting stage, so that you have time to address the challenge.

Maximizing cash may be a matter of addressing one or more of the following:

▶ reducing direct costs

▶ reducing overheads

▶ reducing staff

▶ improving productivity

▶ increasing sales.

If these options have been addressed but there are still difficulties, provided the business is otherwise healthy, raising additional finance might be an option, e.g.:

▶ bank loans/debt

▶ overdraft

▶ equity

▶ trade sale.

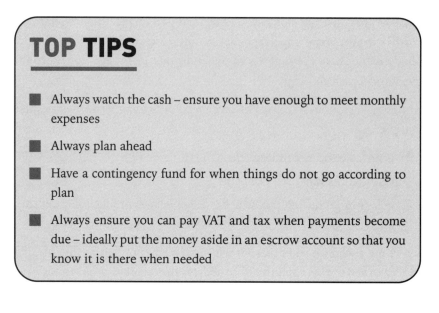

TOP TIPS

■ Always watch the cash – ensure you have enough to meet monthly expenses

■ Always plan ahead

■ Have a contingency fund for when things do not go according to plan

■ Always ensure you can pay VAT and tax when payments become due – ideally put the money aside in an escrow account so that you know it is there when needed

TOO LITTLE FUNDING

It is advisable to include a contingency factor in your estimates for how much money you need to raise. This is for the simple reason that there is a tendency for businesses to underestimate the amount of funding required, and having insufficient funds may impact the long-term survival of your venture.

There is no 'correct' amount which might be used as a contingency, and no single method of determining what you might require – you really have to use your own judgement. One method is to perform a sensitivity analysis, whereby you determine a pessimistic financial model, as well as the one you believe to be most realistic. You can then assess the financial difference, the likelihood of the causes of the more pessimistic scenario occurring etc., and use a suitable factor. Note, however, that if you show a contingency figure which is excessively high, it may give a VC (or other funder) concern that you do not understand your business adequately.

Underestimating your initial funding is unforgivable since, as a start-up, you are beginning with a freshly produced business plan. Having said this, there are an enormous number of things which can go wrong and, to have a contingency for all of them would prove untenable. However the general tip is to ask for too much rather than too little. Indeed a VC would prefer this, since they do not appreciate being asked for additional funding just months after raising an earlier round. Moreover, from your perspective as a shareholder, you may find that your shareholding is diluted more than would otherwise have been the case in any further funding round.

These general remarks also apply to growing businesses where external funding of any type is being raised.

TOP TIPS

- When asking for money from a VC, bank, etc., include a sensible, but justifiable, contingency element

- Do not ask for the absolute minimum funding as determined by the lowest cost business plan scenario. Things will never turn out to be this good in practice. You should prepare a financial sensitivity model (which indicates the required funding in the event that pessimistic forecasts turn out to be the actual outcome) which will help you with your judgements about the size of any contingency element

SPENDING TOO FAST/OVERREACHING

As a general rule spending should be in accordance with the financial projections in your business plan, and there needs to be a very good reason for deviating from it. Spending in excess of your plan without good cause, and without sufficient funds, can be a path to early ruin.

However, there may be cases where spending faster than originally anticipated is permissible. An example might be that your product takes off faster than planned, and you need to increase production. Each case needs to be considered on its merits but whatever the reason, you do need to ensure that at no stage are you actually short of cash in the bank. When you have a good reason for faster spending than planned, a bank overdraft is an extremely useful facility, so speak to your bank manager to see whether he or she can help.

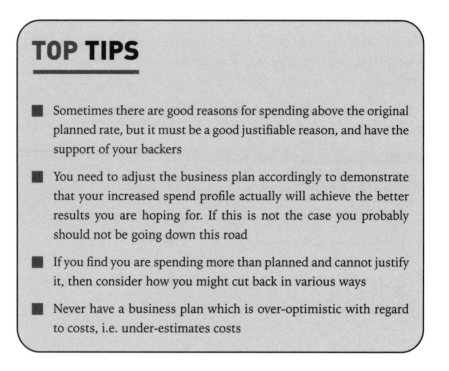

TOP TIPS

- Sometimes there are good reasons for spending above the original planned rate, but it must be a good justifiable reason, and have the support of your backers

- You need to adjust the business plan accordingly to demonstrate that your increased spend profile actually will achieve the better results you are hoping for. If this is not the case you probably should not be going down this road

- If you find you are spending more than planned and cannot justify it, then consider how you might cut back in various ways

- Never have a business plan which is over-optimistic with regard to costs, i.e. under-estimates costs

INVOICING

To be running a business you must have customers. You will be expecting revenues from those customers but, unless you run a cash in hand business, they are only going to actually pay you if they receive an invoice. So prompt issuing of invoices is absolutely essential to maximize cashflow and ensure the health of the business.

Wherever possible, and particularly for smaller operations, if you can obtain your money on completion of your work, or on placement of an order, or delivery of your product, then this is good business. It clearly pays to have a system for producing immediate invoices since you can then more easily ask for payment on delivery.

For larger sums you may be able to arrange phased payments, say, 10% deposit on placement of order, 60% on completion, and the remaining 30% on delivery. Obviously the precise terms and arrangements will vary according to the industry that you are in – but you get the idea.

Larger businesses will have accounts clerks whose job it is to issue invoices. For smaller concerns the task often falls to the business manager, in which case it really is worth the effort to set aside a few minutes each day to do this vital job.

TOP TIPS

■ Always keep on top of your invoicing

■ Try to apply terms whereby you get your money earlier than might otherwise be the case – it will help your cashflow significantly

POOR DEBTOR DAYS

Debtor days is the average number of days your customers take to pay you, the number of days between the date on your invoice and the date the cash appears in your bank account.

As a working principle most businesses have commercial terms and conditions which require payment of any invoice within 30 days. This is a nominal, and the most common, figure. However, many small traders insist on cash on delivery, in which case the debtor days is zero. On the other hand, some businesses may quote a figure somewhat greater than 30 days.

Some customers are absolutely marvellous and pay on receipt of invoice, some are good and meet your terms by paying within the prescribed time (e.g. 30 days). These customers are no problem to you, and are the ones you will undoubtedly have assumed in your business plan. Look after them and make sure you never lose them!

Regrettably there are still many companies which do not believe even in paying by your deadline, and seem to pay either when it suits them, or only after you hassle them. Because the latter category often represents a sizeable proportion of customers, even small companies will benefit from having an accounts clerk whose role includes chasing bad debts.

Monthly review of debtor days by management, ideally at a monthly board meeting, will indicate whether you have a problem with late payers. If the debtor days figure is 30 days or less you probably do not have a problem. If the figure gets to more than 60 days then you should consider having a concerted effort at reducing the figure, and applying pressure on customers to pay up.

It is commonly said that many small firms do not like chasing late payers/bad debts because they feel it might adversely impact the customer–supplier relationship, but this is seldom the case in practice. Any customer has to realize the terms of business. If they are having trouble paying your invoice then they may well be a failing business, in which case you do not need to worry particularly about how they feel. Indeed if they are going to fail you need to put real pressure on them to see if you can get your money before they do actually close down.

Some companies may be late payers either as an internal policy, or because they are just inefficient, or are just so large that their buying and payment functions are completely divorced – creating internal administrative hurdles. For instance, a purchasing manager might have placed the order with you but your invoice may have gone straight to the finance department for payment, and if there are poor communications between the two departments such that there is no appropriate authorization for payment of an invoice, then problems and delays will be all too common.

If you find you are not getting anywhere with your normal contacts in the company which owes you money, you should politely start to escalate the problem through finance managers, to the financial controller, and ultimately to the finance director, if necessary.

If late payment is a real problem you might consider invoice factoring, where you sell your invoices to a factoring company who then take responsibility for collecting payment on your behalf. The downside is that the factoring company only pays you a percentage of the invoice value, often around 90%. This can still be an attractive arrangement for some businesses and can help cashflow considerably, since you get your money as soon as the invoice is presented. However the total costs of this option need to be considered, and what is right for one company may not be right for another.

TOP TIPS

■ Routinely monitor the debtor days figure

■ Take quick action when the figure starts rising

■ Consider invoice factoring as a possibility

■ Take serious action if the debtor day figure rises above double that in your terms and conditions

FINANCIAL RECORDS/BOOK-KEEPING

The simplest way of keeping accounting books these days is to use commercially available software. Software packages for small businesses start at around £150 and are well worth the investment, since they provide so much useful management information.

However, if you are a very small business and/or have an aversion to computers, the very simplest way of keeping accounts is to have four ringbinder files for each of the following, plus a petty cash book:

▶ invoices issued

▶ invoices paid

▶ purchases invoiced

▶ purchases paid.

Each of these files should contain the relevant paperwork/invoice/receipt so at a glance you can determine outstanding payments.

A petty cash book should show what miscellaneous cash purchases have been made, together with copies of all the invoices.

A cash book can then be used to collate the information in each of the files and the petty cash book. This cash book can then be consolidated with your monthly bank statements.

This process is the bare minimum that any business should have by way of accounts books.

The software accounts packages do all of the above automatically, but of course you do need to enter the data on a regular basis (i.e. at least weekly). Note that it is essential that you automatically back up your data at least once a week, to ensure it is not lost. Also note that the use of a software package does not negate the need to store copies of all your receipts and invoices.

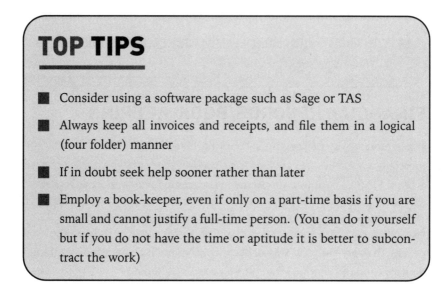

TOP TIPS

■ Consider using a software package such as Sage or TAS

■ Always keep all invoices and receipts, and file them in a logical (four folder) manner

■ If in doubt seek help sooner rather than later

■ Employ a book-keeper, even if only on a part-time basis if you are small and cannot justify a full-time person. (You can do it yourself but if you do not have the time or aptitude it is better to subcontract the work)

AUDITS

All good businesses should have their accounts audited whatever their size. However, small, privately owned businesses with annual revenues below £5.6M (and with a balance sheet of less than £2.8M and fewer than 50 employees) are not legally obliged to have their accounts audited.

Although small companies may be exempted from having their accounts audited there are safeguards in place under company law which protect external shareholders. For instance, Section 249B(2) of the Companies Act 1985 allows shareholders holding at least 10% of the share capital of a company to require an audit of the accounts. Thus you can only avoid an audit completely if there are no external shareholders, or at least none with any significant shareholding.

Businesses which are publicly held/quoted must be audited annually whatever their size.

Auditing for a small business can effectively be undertaken by an accountant who does your annual accounts since, as a third party, they can check the validity of your accounting data, and raise any questions or concerns they might have.

A publicly quoted company should have their annual accounts audited by an accountancy firm different to that which prepared the accounts (assuming they were done outside the company). If there is anything which the auditor is unhappy with, they can qualify their statement regarding the acceptability of the accounts or, in extreme cases, refuse to sign them off completely.

It is important to note that:

▶ the accounts are the responsibility of and should be prepared by management, not the auditors

▶ the auditors should be totally independent from management

▶ the auditors' task is to confirm with reasonable assurance that:

– the financial accounts are free from material misstatement

– the financial data brings out anything that is material to the understanding of the financial accounts and directors' report

▶ the auditors will make their report and state whether they believe:

– the accounts represent a 'true and fair view of the financial position of the company'

– the report and accounts have been prepared in accordance with the relevant parts of the Companies Act 1985

▶ audits provide a high, although not absolute, level of assurance – due to the inherent limitations of the audit procedures normally used (i.e. only a sample of transactions are checked).

Finally, audits should be seen as a good thing in that they provide:

▶ an independent check on management and the company's affairs

▶ useful independent feedback to management regarding their approach to running the business (to the extent that they impact on the audit) and on the effectiveness of internal controls

▶ an independent report which gives comfort to banks, the tax authorities, and both existing and future investors.

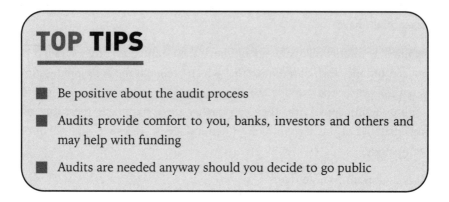

TOP TIPS

■ Be positive about the audit process

■ Audits provide comfort to you, banks, investors and others and may help with funding

■ Audits are needed anyway should you decide to go public

FILING ACCOUNTS AND TAX RETURNS

Whenever you are preparing accounts and tax returns, check the HMRC (Her Majesty's Revenue and Customs) website for the latest information – see Appendix 5. The following categories outline reporting and tax requirements.

Self-employed/sole traders/self-employed partners

Sole traders and partners in partnerships are classified as self-employed. As a self-employed person you have to pay tax on your business profits and any other income. Your accounts do not need to be sent to Companies House, however they are needed so that the appropriate amount of tax can be determined and levied. Hence your accounts need to be finalized and your tax return submitted to HMRC by the end of January following the tax year in question. (NB: these dates are subject to change following announcements in the 2006 Budget – check the HMRC website for latest information – see Appendix 5.). If you have registered with HMRC as being self-employed, in addition to the standard core tax return (SA100) you also have to complete supplementary pages (known as SA103) so as to provide details of your business income and expenses.

For the tax year 2005/2006 tax payments for the self-employed are made in three stages:

1   A first payment on account by 31st January during the tax year. This is normally calculated as 50% of your previous year's tax.

2   A second payment on account has to be paid by 31st July following the end of the tax year. The amount is the same as for the first payment.

3   A final balancing payment (or repayment) is made by 31st January following the tax year in question.

Sole traders can employ staff, contrary to general opinion, and if you do, you need to operate a Pay as You Earn (PAYE) payroll system, and make the necessary returns and payments.

Partnerships

If you are a limited liability partnership then the arrangements are the same as for a limited liability company (see below).

If you are a non-limited liability partnership then the arrangements for each partner are as for the self-employed (see above).

Limited liability companies

As a limited liability company you must prepare a set of accounts. If you have revenues in excess of £5.6M p.a. then the accounts must be audited by an independent auditor.

These accounts must be approved by the board, and sent to Companies House within ten months of the company's accounting reference date (ARD). The accounting reference date is the end of the month in which the company was first registered (unless otherwise altered) and for many businesses, for convenience, is often the same as the end of its financial year.

Table 4.2 gives the deadlines for key submissions and tax payments for a UK limited liability (Ltd) company.

Table 4.2   Deadlines for a limited company (Ltd)

	Form No.	Deadline	Deadline for company whose accounting reference date and financial year end is 31st December
Companies House annual return	363	1 month after ARD	31st January
Payment of Companies House annual registration fee		1 month after ARD	31st January
Annual accounts submitted to Companies House		10 months after ARD	30th October
Corporation tax payable	CT 603	9 months after financial year end – for estimated amount. Over or under payments due following submission of CT return within 12 months of financial year end	30th September
Corporation tax submission	CT 600	12 months after financial year end	31st December

(Source: Data derived from Companies House and HMRC websites for tax year 2005/2006; dates subject to change; ARD = accounting reference date.)

Public limited companies

As a start-up you are unlikely to be set up as a public limited company, since the costs of formation are higher and the requirements more stringent than for a limited liability company.

The submissions to Companies House are made with reference to the company's accounting reference date (ARD). This is normally determined as being at the end of the month after the actual date of incorporation. For instance, if the date of original incorporation was 16th June, then the accounting reference date is 30th June each year.

Note that these dates are subject to change and you should check for the latest on deadlines on the Companies House website.

Table 4.3 gives the deadlines for key submissions and tax payments for a UK public limited company (Plc).

Table 4.3 Deadlines for a public limited company (Plc)

	Form No.	Deadline	Deadline for company whose accounting reference date and financial year end is 31st December
Companies House Annual Return	363	1 month after ARD	31st January
Payment of Companies House annual registration fee		1 month after ARD	31st January
Annual accounts submitted to Companies House		7 months after ARD	31st July
Corporation tax payable	CT 603	9 months after financial year end – for estimated amount. Over or under payments due following submission of CT Return within 12 months of financial year end	30th September
Corporation tax submission	CT 600	12 months after financial year end	31st December

(Source: Data derived from Companies House and HMRC websites for tax year 2005/2006; dates subject to change; ARD = accounting reference date.)

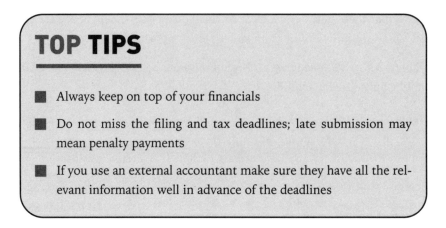

TOP TIPS

- Always keep on top of your financials
- Do not miss the filing and tax deadlines; late submission may mean penalty payments
- If you use an external accountant make sure they have all the relevant information well in advance of the deadlines

TAXATION

Tax rates are subject to change so you are advised to check the HMRC website for the latest information – see Appendix 5 for details.

Taxation for companies

On formation you need to advise HMRC of the company details, etc., so that they have a record of your company on their database.

Income tax (Inland Revenue)

As an employer you have to pay the employees' income tax on their behalf direct to HMRC each month. It is therefore essential that income tax monies withheld from employees' pay packets be kept separate from the rest of the company's money, so that it is available when it has to be paid to the HMRC on the appointed date each month. There will be serious consequences for non-payment, so it is just not worth even getting into such a situation.

The amount due to the HMRC will be worked out as part of the overall payroll calculations, which you can do yourself manually or by using commercially available payroll software or, using an external specialist payroll company.

National Insurance

As for income tax the employer deducts the employees' National Insurance contribution for employees with salaries in excess of a defined minimum (£94 per week in 2006/2007 tax year) at a defined rate (currently 11% in the 2006/2007 tax year) up to the higher tax rate band (£630 per week in the 2006/2007 tax year) and 1% thereafter, and pays the aggregated amount for all employees to the HMRC once a month. In addition the employer has to pay the employer's National Insurance contribution in respect of each employee (12.8% of gross salary in 2006/2007 tax year).

These aggregated amounts can be significant, and to default on payment is not recommended. So, come pay-day, it is recommended that all monies due to the HMRC be put in an escrow account so that you know it is there when it has to be paid.

Corporation tax

Corporation tax is charged on company profits (limited liability companies, public limited companies, and limited liability partnerships if set up as a company), hence the need for the accounts to be produced in good time so that the amount of corporation tax due can be identified and paid on the required date. Note that corporation tax is payable ten months after the end of the financial year (for limited companies) even though the accounts only have to be submitted 12 months after the financial year end.

Corporation tax is not payable by the self-employed, but does apply to the following organizations, even though they are not limited companies:

- ▶ members' clubs, societies and associations
- ▶ trade associations
- ▶ housing associations
- ▶ groups of individuals carrying on a business but not as a partnership (e.g., co-operatives).

VAT (Value Added Tax)

If your revenues or, to use the jargon, taxable supplies, are greater than £60,000 in a year (tax year 2006/2007) then you are obliged to charge VAT on applicable products or services. If your sales are less than this amount you are free to choose whether to charge VAT.

The normal current rate for VAT (2006/2007) is 17.5% on all eligible sales and you have to pay VAT at 17.5% on all eligible purchases (NB: there are some exceptions to the 17.5%).

Most goods are eligible for 17.5% VAT. There are, however, some goods or services which have a 5% rate and some which are zero rated. Further detailed information is available from HMRC (see website details in Appendix 5).

As for the other taxes, the monies collected and due to the HMRC for VAT must be paid on the due date. It is advisable to put these amounts into an escrow account so that you are not tempted to use them for normal operational cashflow purposes.

For small businesses with taxable supplies of less than £150,000 in a year who do not wish to get involved with the VAT paperwork, there is a flat rate scheme whereby you pay a certain percentage of revenues in tax. Owing to the nature of the flat rate scheme some businesses might pay less tax while others might pay more, so the benefit of reducing the paperwork has to be weighed against such considerations.

Taxation for sole traders/self-employed

You need to advise HMRC of your business details, etc., within three months of commencement of trading so that they have a record of your business on their database, and can send you all the appropriate documentation.

Income tax

Tax payments for the self-employed are made in three stages (2005/2006 tax year, but subject to change in future years):

1   A first payment on account by 31st January during the tax year. This is normally calculated as 50% of your previous year's tax.

2   A second payment on account has to be paid by 31st July following the end of the tax year. The amount is the same as for the first payment.

3 A final balancing payment (or repayment) is made by 31st January following the tax year in question.

As a sole trader and/or self-employed person it is essential that income tax monies are put by each month and kept separate from the rest of your finances so that it is available when it has to be paid to HMRC on the appointed date. There will be serious consequences for non-payment so do not get into such a position.

If you employ staff then you will have to collect income tax that they are obliged to pay and make payments as necessary to HMRC.

The amount due to the HMRC for both yourself and any staff will be calculated as part of the overall payroll calculations, which you can do yourself manually, or using commercially available payroll software, or using an external specialist payroll company.

National Insurance

There are a number of categories of National Insurance contributions (NICs) covering employees, employers and the self-employed. There is also a voluntary category for those wishing to make up their payments. The term 'make up' refers to ensuring that you have paid in a sufficient amount so as to obtain maximum benefits. You can either increase weekly/monthly payments or just pay a lump sum to make up any deficiency.

Class 1 Employees and employers

Class 1 payments are split into employees' and employers' contributions:

▶ **Employees**

▷ **Class 1 primary**
Applicable to employees earning over the minimum earnings threshold.
Employees pay at a single rate (currently 11% in 2005/2006 tax year) up to an upper earnings threshold. Above the upper earnings threshold a lower rate applies (currently 1% in 2005/2006 tax year).
These payments are deducted automatically from employees' gross salaries by employers on a weekly/monthly basis.

▶ **Employers**

  ▶ **Class 1 secondary**

  Employers have to pay a flat rate contribution (currently 12.8% in 2005/2006 tax year) on all gross salaries above the primary earnings threshold. There is no upper earnings threshold. Employers have to make the payments monthly.

  ▶ **Class 1A**

  Payable by the employer based on an employee's benefits in kind, such as a company car, private health insurance etc. It is paid by the employer annually.

  ▶ **Class 1B**

  Payable only by employers who have entered into a PAYE Settlement Agreement with HMRC to account for tax on certain expense payments and benefits.

Class 2 Self-employed

Payable by the majority of self-employed individuals at a flat rate, either weekly, monthly or quarterly. Self-employed people also have to pay Class 4 NICs if applicable – see below.

Class 3 Voluntary

Payable at a flat rate by those who have not paid enough NICs in the past to qualify for certain benefits, such as a state pension.

Class 4 Self-employed

Payable by self-employed individuals who have made a certain amount of profit in a year. Calculated annually using the self-assessment tax return form.

A self-employed person has to pay Class 2 contributions which are a fixed rate (£2.10 per week in the 2006/2007 tax year) plus Class 4 contributions (8% for profits between £4,895 and £32,760 and 1% for profits in excess of £32,760 for the 2006/2007 tax year. There is a small earnings exemption for profits below £4345).

The National Insurance amounts can be quite significant and to default on payment is not recommended! It is recommended that you put all monies due to HMRC in an escrow account so that you know it is there when it has to be paid.

Self-employed people can also employ staff. However, as soon as you do, you need to have a Pay As You Earn (PAYE) payroll system, and make all the necessary returns and payments to HMRC, including National Insurance and income taxes, on behalf of employees.

Corporation tax

No corporation tax is payable as a self-employed person.

VAT (Value Added Tax)

If your revenues are greater than £60,000 in a year (2006/2007 tax year) then you are obliged to charge and pay VAT. If your sales are less than this amount you are free to choose whether to charge and pay VAT.

With VAT you can choose to pay monthly or quarterly.

The normal current rate for VAT is 17.5% on all eligible sales and you have to pay VAT at 17.5% on all eligible purchases (NB: there are some exceptions to the 17.5% rate).

Most goods are eligible for 17.5% VAT. There are however some goods or services which have a 5% rate and some which are zero rated. Further detailed information is available from HMRC (see Appendix 5 for website reference).

If your taxable revenues are less than £150,000 p.a. and you are a small business, the HMRC offers a fixed rate scheme whereby you do not need to calculate the VAT on you purchases and sales and calculate the amount of VAT due, but instead merely calculate the VAT owed by using a defined percentage of your sales. The actual percentage varies in the range of 2 to 13%, and is a function of the business sector in which you operate. For some businesses the flat rate approach may be very attractive, for others not so. Helpfully the HMRC has a rate calculator on its website which shows whether, in your particular circumstances, it is advantageous to enter the flat rate scheme (see HMRC website reference in Appendix 5).

There are also other schemes worth investigating such as the cash accounting scheme, the annual accounting scheme (where you file a return once a year, although you still have to make nine monthly payments together with a tenth balancing payment), and a retail scheme. It is recommended that you visit the HMRC website, or seek professional advice to determine which scheme, if any, is best for your business.

As for the other taxes, the monies collected and due to HMRC for VAT must be paid on the due date. It is therefore advisable to put these monies into an escrow account (preferably a high interest bank account) so that you are not tempted to use them for normal operational cashflow purposes.

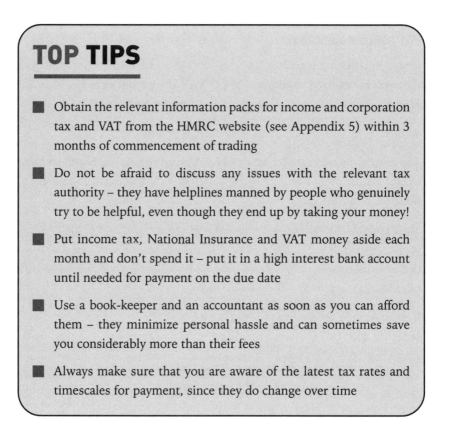

TOP TIPS

■ Obtain the relevant information packs for income and corporation tax and VAT from the HMRC website (see Appendix 5) within 3 months of commencement of trading

■ Do not be afraid to discuss any issues with the relevant tax authority – they have helplines manned by people who genuinely try to be helpful, even though they end up by taking your money!

■ Put income tax, National Insurance and VAT money aside each month and don't spend it – put it in a high interest bank account until needed for payment on the due date

■ Use a book-keeper and an accountant as soon as you can afford them – they minimize personal hassle and can sometimes save you considerably more than their fees

■ Always make sure that you are aware of the latest tax rates and timescales for payment, since they do change over time

PRICING STRATEGY

There are two basic pricing strategies:

1 **Market pricing**

With market pricing you look at the prices being charged in the market generally for your products and services. You then have to decide whether to:

- charge more than the market rate, which may be feasible if your products and services are of higher quality
- charge less than the market rate if, for instance, you are looking to gain market share quickly
- charge the same as the market rate.

While any of these approaches may be justified in any particular instance you should, whichever approach you decide to adopt, just check that the gross margin (gross profit) is sufficient for you to trade profitably in the long term.

2 **Cost-based pricing**

With this approach you take the basic cost of your product or service and determine the selling price by using a predetermined mark-up factor. For instance if you buy a product in at £50 and decide to use a 100% mark-up then the selling price will be £100. This is equivalent to a gross margin of 50%.

It is important to always be clear as to whether you are talking about mark-up or margin, since clearly there is a big difference, and to get the distinction wrong could be disastrous for your business.

When using cost-based pricing the actual mark-up you adopt will vary considerably from product to product and from industry to industry. For instance in a retail shop the mark-up may vary from as little as 5% up to 100% depending on the type of product. Other businesses, which use market pricing, may use margins of anything up to 50 to 60% (and sometimes even more).

If you are just starting out, the mark-up to apply, or margin to aim for (depending on the pricing strategy adopted), is going to be critical to the long term success of your business, and in any business plan it is a fundamental parameter which can make all the difference to success or failure. Ideally, if you have previously worked in the industry or marketplace, then you should know the going rates. If you don't know them, then you need to find out what they are, which is obviously a very delicate exercise, since your prospective competitors are hardly likely to willingly divulge such information.

TOP TIPS

■ Make sure your mark-up or margins are sufficient for your long-term business profitability

■ Make sure your pricing is right for the market you are addressing – so that your products/services will sell

■ Obtain information about the 'going rates' for selling prices, mark-ups and margins

COST BASE

Your cost base comprises two elements:

1   direct costs

These are the direct costs of the product or service, for example manufacture of product (materials and direct production labour), etc.

2   indirect (or overhead) costs

These are all the extra costs involved in the business, such as sales and marketing, management, accommodation, professional fees, etc.

Why is your cost base important? Because if it is too high you will not make enough, if any, profit and your business will be unlikely to survive in the long term. It follows therefore that most companies generally spend a lot of time and effort on minimizing their cost base.

For manufacturers, it means putting pressure on suppliers to reduce prices, and to use more cost-effective manufacturing processes and designs. For service companies it means using the lowest cost base possible, by minimizing accommodation and staff costs, for instance.

The indirect costs are to your own account, and you need to do some internal analysis to check that they are as low as they reasonably can be, consistent with achieving your business goals.

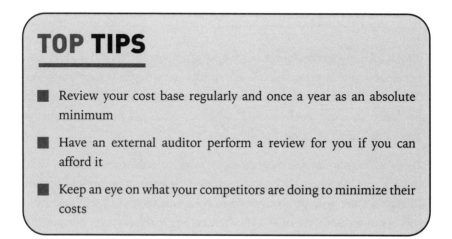

TOP TIPS

- Review your cost base regularly and once a year as an absolute minimum
- Have an external auditor perform a review for you if you can afford it
- Keep an eye on what your competitors are doing to minimize their costs

CONTINGENCY FUND

By now you will have picked up on the theme that in business you will be very lucky if everything runs completely smoothly all the time, and in accordance with your business plan. It is, for most, a fact of life that things will go wrong from time to time.

When difficulties occur, they often have a habit of having financial ramifications. For this reason, as soon as you can reasonably afford to do so, you would be well advised to create a contingency fund (which some call a 'rainy day' account). Such a 'pot of gold' has been of immense value to businesses, both large and small, over the years, and helped them to overcome all manner of hurdles. Obviously such funds should be readily available kept, for instance, in a high interest bearing bank account.

If you are unable to derive a reasonable contingency figure by any other means you might consider simply allocating say, 10% of projected revenues as a contingency fund.

ROLLING FORECASTS

What is a rolling forecast and why might it be important? A rolling forecast is simply a projection (forecast) for a defined period ahead taken at regular intervals. So, for instance, in January you might look at sales forecasts for the next 12 months up to the end of December. However in February, the 12-month rolling forecast will look at sales from February until the end of the next January.

Why is this inspection of rolling forecasts important? It is because many businesses have a cyclical nature with peaks and troughs throughout a year. On top of this there are spurious external influences which can make a big difference to sales, such as interest rates, etc., and to costs – such as changes in the price of oil.

It is not uncommon for businesses to produce a 12 month/annual P&L forecast and to rigorously review performance against budget each month throughout the year up to the end of their financial year, e.g. December. This is fine except that, unless they use rolling forecasts, it is not until the end of the year that they start to look at sales in the next January and beyond. By this time there could be dramatic changes in sales projections, which the 12-month-old plan could not foresee. But with a rolling forecast any external influences can be identified as and when they start to occur, and solutions adopted to mitigate the situation well ahead of time.

TOP TIPS

- Always use 12-month rolling forecasts wherever possible
- Keep abreast of all developments which might impact on sales and costs over a 12-month cycle

USE OF KEY PERFORMANCE PARAMETERS AND RATIOS

This book has previously mentioned the importance of regularly monitoring the performance of the business and it is very convenient to use key performance parameters and ratios to do this on a month-to-month basis. The key parameters that might be used for any given business will vary. The following are examples of some key parameters which will apply to most, if not all, businesses:

1 **Cash burn in month**

   'Cash burn' is simply the term used to denote the amount of cash being spent, typically per month. It is important because knowing the cash burn, you can determine how solvent the business is and, in particular, when it is likely to run out of money. You can then ensure you act in sufficient time to plug the 'funding gap'. Note that it is unlawful to trade insolvently, i.e. without the ability to pay your bills as they become due, with serious consequences for directors involved, so this is very important information.

2 **Cash in hand**

   Note how it is varying month by month and if going down, whether this is according to plan or possibly an indication of impending problems. For start-ups with no immediate revenues it is recommended that you monitor the date when the cash is likely to run out, so that you can take timely action to avoid trading insolvently.

3 **Creditors cash ratio**

$$\frac{\text{Amount creditors are owed}}{\text{Amount of readily available funds, i.e. cash}}$$

   If the ratio is greater than one then you are possibly wrongfully trading. Wrongful trading is when you have insufficient funds to pay your creditors. If you think you are wrongfully trading then you need to take urgent action, possibly putting the company into administration or liquidation. You should seek urgent specialist advice.

4 **Sales vs budget**

   This should be reviewed ideally with the following sub-analysis:

> sales in month compared with budget

> cumulative sales in year to date versus budget

> forecast end of year sales versus budget forecast for full year

> forecast sales for next 12 months (i.e. rolling forecast)

5 **Staff turnover (churn)**

This is the percentage of staff who have left, divided by the total work-force. It can be measured on a monthly basis, year to date basis, or on a rolling annual basis. Figures can be typically in the range of 5 to 20%. See also p. 86.

6 **Sales per employee**

This is sales divided by the number of employees, best measured on an annual basis, and one of a number of measures of productivity. This parameter varies considerably according to industry and even within a sector. For instance some high-tech businesses selling high value prod-ucts/services can have sales per employee approaching £500,000, whereas many low-tech manufacturing businesses may have sales per employee of as little as £50,000.

7 **Gross margin**

This is the margin available for overheads, profit, etc. Calculated as a percentage by subtracting direct (e.g. manufacturing) costs from sales, and then dividing by total sales. The gross margin you should be look-ing for varies according to the industry you are operating in. Some high-tech industries can achieve gross margins of as much as 60 to 70%, whereas some shops achieve as little as 5% (although they may have high sales volumes to compensate).

8 **Profit margin**

This measures profit divided by sales. When considered in conjunction with gross margin it indicates whether overhead costs are at an accept-able level. Profit margins of anything between 5 to 30% might be tar-geted, but once again what might actually be achievable will vary from sector to sector.

9 **Customer satisfaction**

Customer satisfaction is a measure of the satisfaction which a customer has with the product/service. It tends to be a subjective measure but, because businesses recognize the importance of keeping customers satisfied/happy, they try to quantify it as best they can. It is often measured by canvassing customers and/or obtaining customer feedback in some way, quantifying the results, and usually expressing the result as a percentage.

10 Customers lost in month

(Can be presented as a percentage of total customers.)

Obviously this is usually a bad news measure. The only time when it is a good news measure is when you have decided to strategically focus on a smaller number of high revenue generating customers, and can reduce your costs and increase your profits as a result.

11 Customers gained in month/average total number of customers

(Can be presented as a percentage of total customers.)

The purpose of this measure is to determine, as a minimum, that you are not losing customers. If for instance, you are investing in increased sales activity or a new product, then you can readily assess the effect that your increased sales and marketing activity is having on the number of customers.

TOP **TIPS**

- Using key performance indicators is a very useful method of assessing the month-to-month performance of a company

- If in doubt about which indicators to use seek professional help from, for instance, your accountant or other business advisor

INVESTMENT APPRAISAL

A business uses the technique of investment appraisal to assess whether it can afford to make a purchase, and to evaluate and compare various offerings and financing strategies. A purchase can be either a piece of machinery or even another business. This book cannot go into the various techniques for investment appraisal, which can be quite complex. However, it is important to note that, getting an investment appraisal wrong can, in extreme cases, be disastrous, so it is very important to fully understand what you are doing.

Appraisals will take account of numerous factors such as cost of acquisition, operating costs, interest rates, production capability, etc. Some of these factors will be well defined and fixed, others will be estimates, and others inspired guesses. Suffice to say that getting the less well-defined factors wrong by very much can alter the investment decision dramatically.

In any business calculation where a project or investment occurs over a period of time, let us say in excess of a year, then there is a need to take into account the 'time value of money'. What this means is that:

1   you could just put the money into an interest bearing bank account and the money would grow if the interest was reinvested each time it was paid and

2   inflationary pressures mean that £100 now will not buy as much in 5 years' time.

In performing investment appraisals and the like it is vitally important that the time value of money is included in the calculations. Getting these figures badly wrong can bring about a company's demise, especially if the numbers are large and the company is small. It is therefore also very important to perform a sensitivity analysis – to 'flex' the numbers – so that you can assess the downsides if certain things were to happen, for instance a steep rise in interest rates.

Common investment appraisal techniques are discounted cash flow (DCF) and internal rate of return (IRR).

Discounted cash flow is the technique that analyzes what you might pay today in order to benefit from anticipated cash flow in years to come. In practice it means that any cash flows in future years must be discounted in order to determine their present day values.

By way of example, if inflation is assumed to be 5%, mathematical tables can be used to show that the value of any investment would reduce by around 22% over 5 years. Using DCF you can compare various investment decisions and determine which is the most attractive investment option.

You are advised to seek advice from your accountant or other business advisor if you are not familiar with the techniques. Some of the books listed in Appendix 5 give more information on investment appraisal.

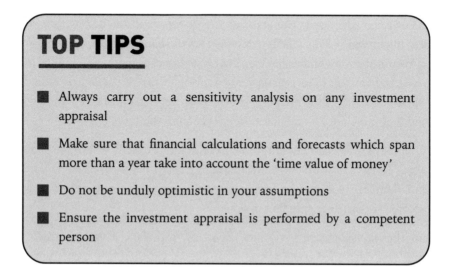

TOP TIPS

- Always carry out a sensitivity analysis on any investment appraisal
- Make sure that financial calculations and forecasts which span more than a year take into account the 'time value of money'
- Do not be unduly optimistic in your assumptions
- Ensure the investment appraisal is performed by a competent person

FOREIGN CURRENCY AND SALES

Businesses buying products and services from abroad, or selling to foreign countries, encounter a particular additional set of potential problems in the form of foreign currency and exchange rate fluctuations.

The clever solution would be if a British importer or exporter could trade in its local currency, e.g. sterling, for all its transactions. Indeed this can happen for some countries and some products, e.g. oil imports into the USA, because oil is traded internationally in US dollars. However, for most importers, commercial agreements to buy from a foreign business are very likely to be in the seller's foreign currency. Accordingly you, as the purchaser, have to pay in that currency.

Unfortunately few currencies are fixed or linked to others, and many are traded in foreign exchange markets, such that the exchange rate with the pound may vary over time. This means that if the foreign currency goes down relative to the pound, the product or service you are buying may become more expensive, whereas if the rate goes up then the cost of importing will decrease.

Small foreign exchange variations can usually be factored into your business calculations. However, if you have a long-term contract, spanning maybe more than a year, then there is a significant currency risk which needs to be addressed. The usual way to do this is through your bank, by 'buying forward'. This means agreeing with the bank that at a certain time in the future you will be able to exchange an agreed number of pounds for an agreed amount of foreign currency. Obviously the bank takes account of whether it believes the exchange rate in question is likely to go up or down, and it also includes its costs for the provision of the service.

What buying forward does mean is that you know exactly where you stand with regard to how much you will have to pay at the agreed payment date, and therefore you will at least know your profit will not be adversely affected by exchange rate fluctuations.

Another consideration if you are exporting, especially if you are trading with less developed countries, is what happens if there are events which prevent you from receiving payment, for instance, a war, civil unrest, political instability, etc. The UK Government offers an export credit guarantee service through the Export Credit Guarantee Department (ECGD), part of the Department of Trade and Industry, which underwrites some or all of the monies due to your company in the event of one of the stated 'risk' events occurring. Most developed countries offer similar services to their exporters.

TOP TIPS

- If buying from abroad, and the purchase spans some period of time, then consider buying your foreign currency on a 'buying forward' basis. Consult your bank who will advise on each particular case

- If exporting consider obtaining an export credit guarantee from the ECGD

LOANS (DEBT)

Loans (or debt) are normal in business, and many businesses will take on debt to grow and expand, to make an acquisition, etc. Sole traders and self-employed people will also, more often than not, find that they need to take out loans to finance their business. The important thing to remember is to only take on loans where you can afford the monthly repayments.

If either you personally, or the business, are having trouble with the loan repayments and there is a danger of the business going under, then in an effort to avoid losing their money the bank may offer to extend the loan period. Where the amount of debt is not being increased this has the effect of reducing the monthly payments, which may help your cashflow considerably.

Alternatively, if the loan amount is increased, it may mean that you still pay around the same monthly amount but have the benefit of immediate additional free cash, which could perhaps be used to pay creditors, etc.

Debt *per se* is not a problem. The problems occur when there is some difficulty in repaying the loan.

If the business is not producing sufficient cash to make even the extended repayments then you have to start to consider whether you are ever going to be in a position to repay the loan.

A common characteristic of virtually all entrepreneurs is that they are optimists; indeed they usually need to be to get a venture off the ground. However there comes a time, if you are experiencing money problems, when reality must temper the optimism. It is always tempting to say your sales are about to grow dramatically and everything will then be rosy, and sometimes this is indeed the case. But miracles do not happen too often in the real world and it is important to be realistic. The moral is not to pour good money after bad.

One of the most useful things you can do when you start to experience problems is to share them with others, especially professional people who may have been in the situation themselves, or accountants who can give advice. A third party view of your situation and the prospects for success can prove tremendously helpful.

You are always well advised to keep your bank manager informed of your financial position. However be aware that, in today's climate, bank managers are just like most businesspeople in having to achieve their targets and, as a consequence, can be willing to offer to extend loans, or even give new loans, when in reality there is little prospect of the business coming good and you being able to make even the new repayments. It is therefore important to make your own decisions and maybe obtain a second opinion before proceeding.

Larger loans will be secured, often on your house or, for a larger company, on some of your capital assets such as plant or machinery, or buildings if you own them. If you default on your payments then the bank, with a charge on the asset, can force you to sell it against your wishes. If the charge is on your house you might be able to obtain a remortgage to fund the debt, but even this is only sensible if you can realistically expect to be able to personally pay the new monthly repayments. Remember also that, with a mortgage, you are effectively just spreading the loan over a longer period, typically 25 years. This may not be a problem if your business is successful and takes off so that you can repay some, or all, of the mortgage early, but you may be compounding your problems if the business is not as successful as planned.

TOP **TIPS**

■ Do not take on loans that you cannot afford to repay

■ In assessing what size loan you can take on consider a worse case scenario and work out how you might repay the loans in such circumstances

■ Share you problems with a third party who can give you impartial advice, maybe your accountant or a business friend or mentor

PERSONAL TAXATION

Why mention personal taxation in a business book? The answer is, mainly for the benefit of anyone not paying tax through the Pay As You Earn (PAYE) tax system, which can include sole traders/self-employed, as well as some directors of companies.

The income tax arrangements for the self-employed are given on p. 50. The point to note is that income tax for the self-employed has to be paid in three separate instalments, with a large amount (50%) payable by the end of January of the current tax year, and the other two payments in stages by the end of the following January (NB: these deadlines may be subject to change). It is very easy to forget about these payments and therefore very easy to spend the tax money, the result being that the pot is empty come the time to pay up!

The advice has to be, therefore, to pretend you are on PAYE and put an appropriate amount of money aside into a high interest bearing bank account each month, so that the money is there for when the tax is due for payment. If in doubt about how much to set aside, ask your accountant to calculate the amount for you. This has to be a sensible approach, and will relieve you of a great deal of anxiety, and allow you to sleep easy at night, knowing that at least you shouldn't be having problems with paying tax.

The same philosophy applies to company directors in cases where you may not be paying tax via PAYE, e.g. where you are not an employee. You should calculate the tax due on your drawings, usually dividend payouts, and put the money aside in a high interest bank account. The plus side is that at least you benefit from some interest until the tax bill arrives.

Unfortunately HMRC is not very forgiving about non-payment of tax and insists on payment with interest if the bill is not paid on time. For many this can be the last straw, especially if the business has not progressed as well as had originally been envisaged.

TOP TIPS

- Put tax due aside on a monthly basis in an escrow account

PERSONAL CAPITAL GAINS

As an entrepreneur starting out you do not normally consider the issues surrounding selling off the business downstream. However, if you have been successful and have grown the business over a period of time, you may find that either:

1   you wish to float the company on the full stock exchange, or maybe AIM (Alternative Investment Market, a junior market of the stock exchange) or

2   you decide to sell to a trade buyer, or perhaps a competitor makes an attractive offer for the acquisition of your company or

3   maybe you just wish to retire and sell to a trade buyer, or your management team wants to buy the company via the mechanism of a management buy out (MBO).

On successful completion of a flotation, or trade sale, you will hopefully find yourself with a lot of money in your bank account. Unfortunately HMRC thinks that a goodly proportion of this money should be paid to it as capital gains tax. however, there are what are known as 'taper reliefs', which vary according to whether the capital gain goes to a company or an individual, and is a function of how long the 'asset' which brought about the capital gain has been held. The longer the better as far as taper relief is concerned. Suffice to say the best way of minimizing capital gains tax on an exit is best planned well ahead of the exit date, and it is always best to obtain the advice of a specialist tax accountant on these matters.

TOP TIPS

■ If you are approaching an exit then seek expert advice at the earliest opportunity. The advice will cost you money but the experts will probably save you many times the amount spent

PERSONAL GUARANTEES

Simple advice – do not give personal guarantees if you can possibly avoid it. If you cannot avoid it only guarantee what you can afford to lose!

It is very common for a start-up, when buying something on a hire purchase or similar contract, and where there is no credit history, for one or more directors (or the proprietor in the case of a sole trader) to be asked to provide personal guarantees in the event that there is a default by the company on payments due.

You may have various individual contracts, each of which is personally guaranteed, and may each be relatively small in financial terms, but you need to recognize that if the company defaults, or in extreme cases liquidates, then all the contracts will become due simultaneously. You may end up with an enormous bill, which you are obliged to pay (because you provided personal guarantees) and which you may not be able to afford, with the result that you personally might be made bankrupt.

This is particularly the case if you are not a limited company, but directors of limited companies can be in just as much trouble if they have provided personal guarantees.

TOP **TIPS**

■ Don't guarantee or underwrite any amount of money that you cannot afford to lose (here is the voice of experience!)

FUNDING SOURCES

There are two main sources of funding, namely equity and debt, which are discussed below. Every source of external funding will need to see some form of business plan, which has to be acceptable to them, before they commit any funds (see Chapter 3).

Equity

Equity means the funder takes a stake in the business, i.e. becomes a shareholder, in return for providing a given amount of money. Also be aware that, over time, you may wish to raise further equity funds (known in the jargon as a further 'round' of funding). However, each new tranche of funding means that each new equity funder will want a stake in the company. The net effect is that your personal stake becomes diluted over time, i.e. reduces. This sounds like bad news but in practice, for most growing companies, the valuation of the company should have increased each time you go for further equity funding such that, even though you might personally have a smaller stake in percentage terms, in money terms, your stake will have increased.

There are a number of sources of equity finance:

1   **Family and friends**

    This may be the easiest and cheapest source of funding. Given that this category is under the equity heading it means that the relative or friend is savvy enough to want a slice of the action by taking a shareholding.

2   **Business angels**

    Business angels are typically high net worth people who have substantial sums of money at their disposal, and who are prepared to invest some of it in businesses, and especially start-ups. They vary as to how demanding they may be in terms of the stake they require; they may also wish to participate in the running of the company, and have a seat on the board, which is not always a bad thing if they have valuable experience to bring to the business. Individual business angels may be prepared to invest anything between £10,000 and £500,000, although a typical average figure is around £50,000. It is not uncommon, where a business is looking for funding of up to around £1M, for business angels to join forces to raise the full amount required. Depending on the funding sought they may take up to around a 50% stake in the company, and sometimes even more.

There are various websites which give information about finding business angels including Business Link, and the National Business Angel Network, or alternatively your professional advisors may also be able to recommend locally based angels (see Appendix 5 for further information).

3   Venture capital

Companies looking to raise more than c.£1M probably need to investigate venture capital funding, although there are some VCs who will provide seed and early stage funding of less than £1M. Certainly the larger VCs will not entertain funding anything below £1–5M and some will not even consider start-ups, preferring to invest only in well-established companies with a revenue and profit history upon which they can make judgements about future growth. More detailed information about venture capital funding is given in Chapter 16.

The best source of information about venture capital firms is the British Venture Capital Association website (see Appendix 5 for details).

4   Strategic investors

Strategic investors generally means companies who might be prepared to invest because they operate in your field, but who are not venture capitalists. An example might be a large international software company which might be prepared to invest in some wonderful unique new software which you have developed.

Loans/debt (see also p. 65)

Loans, which are sometimes referred to as debt, are where a bank or other body gives you the money you require and you have to repay the sum, together with interest, over a defined time period. It is the classic method of obtaining money, but it only works if you can afford to make the monthly repayments. If there is some doubt about your ability to make the repayments, then you should not proceed. An independent financial advisor or an accountant can advise you as to the best course of action.

1   The usual source of loans is your local high street bank. They will lend typically up to £20,000 on an unsecured basis, but anything over this would have to be secured against some tangible asset, such as a house. For further information see the websites of the major high street banks.

2   For young people under 30 who need no more than £5,000 to get started, the Prince's Trust might be able to help. The advantage of the Prince's Trust scheme is that the loan comes with a free business consultant and mentor (worth thousands). See Appendix 5 for details of The Prince's Trust website.

Miscellaneous

1   Grants

It is possible to obtain grants from regional development agencies and the DTI for some businesses in certain locations offering particular products or services. The amounts on offer are not normally more than £50,000. Sometimes the grant authority will match the sum of money that you invest.

Further information on sources of grants is available on various websites, details of which are given in Appendix 5.

2   General

Business Link provides a very useful review of all types of funding and their website details can be found in Appendix 5.

TOP **TIPS**

- Don't use other people's money if you can possibly avoid it – this is from the perspective of maintaining control of your business and maximizing your personal shareholder value

- Use other people's money if you have no choice, for instance if the amount to be raised is significant, or if the risks are greater than you can personally bear

- Don't ask for too much or too little when looking to others for funding

- Don't borrow (by way of loans) more than you can afford to pay back

- Be aware that raising equity finance means your stake in the company is diluted, and will be further reduced each time you require further equity financing, albeit offset by the increase in value of the business

5

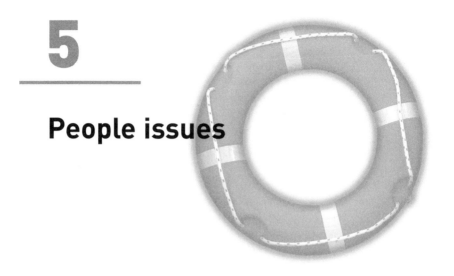

People issues

PEOPLE EMERGENCY PACK

If you are already experiencing people/staffing problems Table 5.1 lists various warning signs, suggests causes, and proposes solutions.

Table 5.1   Some people problem warning signs, causes and solutions

Warning sign	Possible cause	Possible solution
Best/key employees leaving	Morale problem Fears of job losses Staff sensing problems in company	Communicate with staff Ensure staff know the issues Staff can often help address the problem with new ideas, etc. Involve staff and they will be more motivated If situation is not disastrous then ensure staff know what you are doing to address issues
Poor morale	Loss of morale manifested by: – poor timekeeping – staff becoming edgy – fewer after-work drinks	Identify causes of low morale and develop strategy to address it/them

Table 5.1 continued

Warning sign	Possible cause	Possible solution
	– becoming protective of their positions – poor employee participation – poor management	
Low productivity	Poor morale	See above Develop strategy for addressing concerns
Difficulty in recruiting	Company in low unemployment area Low wages offered Company has poor reputation Unexciting work	Ask potential recruits why they are not accepting offers Speak to local job centre
Staff underpaid	Poor morale Low productivity	See above
Staff overpaid	Pay creep	Carry out reassessment of reasonable pay rates and adjust over time
Poor performers	Inadequate training Inadequate management attention	Reassess training programme Ensure management carries out performance reviews and train as necessary
Fraud/theft	Lax management Inadequate security systems Staff underpaid Poor morale	Review security systems Analyze causes Speak to culprits to understand reasons and address accordingly

GENERAL

Companies are made up of people. This is hard to believe if you are a small cog in an enormous corporation but it is true, even though you may not always feel that your efforts are in any way significantly contributing to the greater good of the company.

In smaller companies each employee has to pull their weight, 'hangers-on' cannot usually be tolerated, hence the need for the very best decision making when recruiting your managers and staff.

What is not commonly appreciated is the high level of 'churn' of management in the early years of a start-up. It has been suggested that, especially for VC funded start-ups, as many as 10% of managers might be replaced within the first two years, and almost 40% within around three years.

Of course there is management and staff churn in any company and a certain amount is healthy, in that new blood is introduced. However, to have almost half the management replaced in the first three years or so certainly says something about start-up companies, the people who create them (i.e. the founders), and the selection of their first management team.

Some of the more obvious reasons for this high level of management churn in start-ups are:

1   VCs expecting quick returns and hence requiring the very best management talent.
2   The inability of the company to select (or afford) the best and most appropriate managers, especially in the early growth stages.
3   The fact that the management expertise required in getting a start-up created and running in the first couple of years is often different to that required once the company is established and moving into the maturity growth phase.

So it may be concluded that it is vitally important to recruit the best and most appropriate managers from the outset, in so far as this is possible. Even as a sole trader, if you are looking to grow and employ staff, then the tips in this chapter should prove invaluable.

Recruiting the very best people will go a long way to ensuring a great company, but how do you get great people on board? One of the best ways, especially for start-ups is, wherever possible, to use your own networks of contacts. Identify the positions you need to fill and think, for each vacancy, who do I know in the whole wide world who would be the very best person for the job? This assessment needs to take account not only of their ability to excel at the job, but also of whether they would be a good cultural fit within the company. If you can think of someone who meets the requirements, then meet with them and entice them on board. If you cannot think of a suitable person ask your contacts if they know of anyone.

It is not uncommon to be able to grow a company to as many as 100 staff, just by using your contacts. For start-ups this can lead to an excellent company culture because you know the people, they probably know you, you know that they can do the job and can hit the ground running, and that if they have joined your firm, they are going to be committed to making a success of the venture.

In the internet boom years there were stories of staff joining start-ups for a reduced salary, compensated for by stock options, which they hoped would eventually make them rich. Things have moved on since those heady days and salary packages now have to be realistic. For great people you may have to pay over the odds, but if they are genuinely that good, they may well be worth it.

Using your network of contacts also has the benefit of minimizing recruitment costs, which is bad news for head-hunters and recruitment firms, but good news for your cashflow.

When preparing your business plan it must include accurate assumptions about pay levels, otherwise the costs of running the business before revenues are generated are likely to escalate, i.e. cash-burn could be significantly greater than planned, and the venture could run out of money prematurely. Remember also to allow for the extra costs of employing staff such as taxes, benefits, bonuses, recruitment costs, etc., which can easily add up to an extra 25% on top of the base salary, or even 33% for top staff.

VCs or business angels are never pleased at having to inject more money into a business because you did not get your sums right in the business plan, and they will certainly want to study any updated plan in minute detail. In some circumstances, they may wish to review the management (i.e. the CEO and/or others might be asked to go)!

Recruitment agencies and head-hunters can charge anything up to 30–35% of the first year's salary of the person appointed, which might be fairly trivial for a big company, but can represent an enormous expense for a start-up or other young company. When you do use a recruitment company make sure they operate and have experience in your sector, that they have an excellent relevant database of contacts, and have a complete understanding of the type of person you are looking to recruit. There is nothing worse than paying a recruitment firm or head-hunter and then finding out six months later that you have made a bad choice of candidate, although of course there is nobody to blame but yourself in such circumstances.

You might give some thought to the use of consultants, and/or interim managers, and/or temporary staff, just to get you off the ground. Any good people you come across can be offered a permanent position. This is a very common approach nowadays for recruiting secretaries, and can be applied just as well for other staff.

As your start-up grows it may reach a size where you can justify the appointment of a human resources/personnel manager or director. Such a position should not be entered into lightly, but a good HR manager/director will help management ensure:

▶ a happy, motivated and productive workforce
▶ that the company avoids the legal minefields regarding recruiting and firing staff, as well as ensuring that it complies with all the employment and related rules and regulations for staff at work, e.g. paternity/maternity regulations, etc.

Finally, where the company does have an HR manager/department, managers should never forget that the management of the staff is still their responsibility, not that of the HR department. The HR department is there to advise, implement appropriate HR processes and procedures, etc., and to complement the people management responsibilities of the manager.

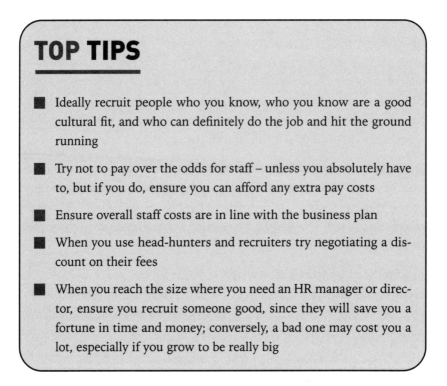

TOP TIPS

■ Ideally recruit people who you know, who you know are a good cultural fit, and who can definitely do the job and hit the ground running

■ Try not to pay over the odds for staff – unless you absolutely have to, but if you do, ensure you can afford any extra pay costs

■ Ensure overall staff costs are in line with the business plan

■ When you use head-hunters and recruiters try negotiating a discount on their fees

■ When you reach the size where you need an HR manager or director, ensure you recruit someone good, since they will save you a fortune in time and money; conversely, a bad one may cost you a lot, especially if you grow to be really big

MANAGEMENT AND LEADERSHIP

Are good leaders/managers born or bred?

As a manager in a start-up you probably wonder about the answer to this question from time to time, especially when you realize that the leadership style of your company will be coming from you.

It has to be recognized that there are some excellent leaders who have never been near a management college. There are also a lot of managers who perhaps have not necessarily been born with great leadership skills, but who can improve them sufficiently so as to be able to successfully lead teams and companies to success. Inevitably there will also be some debate as to what constitutes a good leader/manager.

Some of the qualities of a good leader and manager are listed below.

▶ someone whom everyone respects

▶ someone who knows the job and can achieve results

▶ a good communicator who also listens

▶ sets goals but does not supervise more closely than necessary

▶ encourages and praises (use of carrot rather than stick)

▶ encourages employee participation in decision-making.

To be successful a good manager/leader needs to have most of these qualities. If you want to be successful and currently are not able to demonstrate all these qualities, it would be worth working on those areas where you might be deficient.

Managers who keep missing goals/budgets, etc.

Having managers and staff who keep missing goals/deadlines/budgets is a nightmare for any company, but especially so for start-ups.

It is essential to have measures in place so that you can tell how well your managers and top executives are performing. This generally requires an appraisal system whereby, at the beginning of each year, the company goals and targets are set. These then flow down by department/executive so that individual targets can be assigned such that, if everyone meets their targets, the company performance will be met, and everyone will be happy. This approach can be adopted by even small businesses.

This means the targets set for each individual manager must be related to the overall company targets. Performance against these targets should be reviewed at appropriate intervals, and typically at least six monthly, if not quarterly. The reason for this is that no one should want a manager to underperform. If there are problems of whatever nature, which could mean that the targets might not be met at the end of the year, it is better to be able to address them while there is still a chance of remedial action, or of developing alternative strategies while there is still time, rather than waiting until the end of the year and admitting defeat.

It is a fact of life, however, that some managers may just not be up to the job. If they are clearly continually underperforming, despite managerial help and support, then action will need to be taken since a business cannot survive indefinitely carrying such people, and especially a start-up.

Adopting a formal appraisal process makes identifying the problems that much easier. Difficulties may be due to lots of different reasons. The under-performing manager may have been recruited or promoted beyond their level of competence, or into an area where they have insufficient skills and/or knowledge. A good company will endeavour to address any weak-nesses, but eventually some hard decisions will have to be made regarding any continually underperforming individual.

Poor quality staff or managers can easily be a cause for business failure, especially in smaller businesses where every member of staff has to carry their weight. It is therefore important to recruit the right people at the outset, since the cost of not doing so can be disastrous. The next section discusses the recruitment of key individuals.

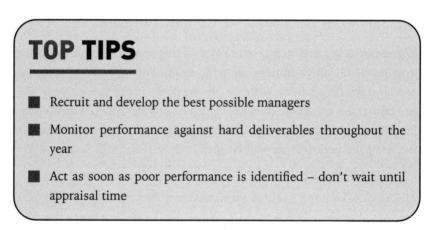

TOP TIPS

- Recruit and develop the best possible managers
- Monitor performance against hard deliverables throughout the year
- Act as soon as poor performance is identified – don't wait until appraisal time

RECRUITMENT – USING HEAD-HUNTERS AND RECRUITMENT AGENCIES

It costs a great deal of money to recruit a new member of staff, sometimes up to 33% of the first year's salary, and this of course excludes your time in preparing job descriptions, interviewing, and all the administrative behind-the-scenes work. The choice of a recruitment company is critical, since they vary a lot. As always it is best to use a company which has expert-ise in your field and who comes recommended by someone whose advice you respect.

You can, of course, do everything yourself, which can be somewhat cheaper, although is time-consuming administratively in that you have to prepare and place adverts, sift responses, arrange initial weeding interviews, etc. If you feel up to the task, know where best to advertise and are prepared for the administrative chores, it is not necessarily a bad route, especially for a cash strapped start-up.

To dismiss someone can be expensive, not only because you have to go through the recruitment process again but also, if the dismissal process is not carried out appropriately, the company could face legal action for a variety of different reasons, including wrongful dismissal, unfair dismissal, etc.

The answer then is to do your level best to recruit the right person for the job first time around. The selection process should not therefore be delegated to those without experience, or who may not be involved with the new recruit once appointed. The job should never be left just to the HR department. However, you do need some knowledge of legislation as it relates to recruitment, for instance there are certain things which you cannot say at an interview, especially if they are of a discriminatory nature, and advice from an HR department, or HR advisor, should be sought before proceeding with any interview for the first time.

Unfortunately, it has to be recognized that interviews are not as perfect a method of finding the right recruit as one might hope. There is a belief that there is a 50:50 chance that you will recruit a good member of the team, purely using interview techniques. This also assumes the interviewers have some experience and a track record of success in appointing good staff. Notwithstanding this, most staff are still recruited using interviews. However, there are a few things that you can do to put the balance in your favour:

1   Recruit someone you or a colleague already know, who you can be sure can do the job, and who will be a good cultural fit. It sounds a bit like nepotism, but it pays dividends.

2   Do not rely on an interview alone. Get the interviewee to do a test which will illustrate their capability in the prospective job. Aptitude tests are also sometimes useful, although even these are by no means perfect.

3   Obtain a meaningful reference. You have to proceed with great caution here in that, if you write for a reference, you are unlikely to obtain the information which you really need to know. In an ideal world the best way would be to speak to the prospective employee's existing (or previous) manager, and ask pointed questions such as, 'Would you hire this person again?' The problem with this approach is that it is inappropriate to obtain such a reference before a job offer has been made, since their current employer may not be aware of the person's desire to leave. If the reference is such that the job offer is withdrawn then the prospective employee is left in an extremely invidious position in their current company. Another, perhaps better, although more costly approach is to use a head-hunter to contact people in the prospective employee's existing company, whereby they can usually obtain quite a good pen portrait of the target candidate.

4   Have the employment contract incorporate a trial period of three to six months, with performance reviews throughout this period. Although it is bad news for the new recruit if they are asked to leave at the end of the trial period, at least you are not left with having to employ someone who is not up to the job, and you can avoid unwanted litigation.

Given the above you can see why recruiting people you already know is an attractive approach, and using professional HR experts in any recruitment helps ameliorate the angst!

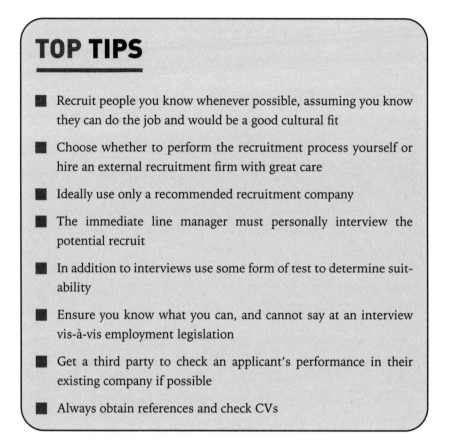

TOP **TIPS**

- Recruit people you know whenever possible, assuming you know they can do the job and would be a good cultural fit

- Choose whether to perform the recruitment process yourself or hire an external recruitment firm with great care

- Ideally use only a recommended recruitment company

- The immediate line manager must personally interview the potential recruit

- In addition to interviews use some form of test to determine suitability

- Ensure you know what you can, and cannot say at an interview vis-à-vis employment legislation

- Get a third party to check an applicant's performance in their existing company if possible

- Always obtain references and check CVs

KEY MANAGERS/STAFF LEAVING

One major cause of difficulty, especially for smaller firms, is that they tend to be dependent on key workers. If one or more of those key members of staff leave, for whatever reason, the company can be in serious trouble. Invariably in small companies, and especially high-tech type operations, there will be a caucus of indispensable members of staff who are not readily replaceable. If any one of these key people leaves the company there can be major consequential problems such as:

- ▶ delays to development programmes
- ▶ delays in product development/manufacture
- ▶ delays in customer payments (i.e. sales) and hence impact on cashflow.
- ▶ reduced sales, etc.

The possible solutions are not that difficult to deploy:

▶ look after all your staff, but especially key staff who you just cannot afford to lose

▶ make staff feel wanted. Studies have indicated that this is even more important than financial reward, and yet it costs the company little

▶ pay them well, but note that money is not everything

▶ offer stock options (if really necessary)

▶ offer other benefits

▶ determine their hot buttons – sometimes the reasons for leaving are not monetary. Find out what makes your key staff tick and most likely to want to stay, and make it happen

▶ although it may be a case of closing the stable door after the horse has bolted, key person insurance may at least mitigate the financial problems when an important member of staff departs.

TOP TIPS

■ Maximize morale

■ Make staff at all levels feel wanted and praise them when they do well

■ If you, or managers, are not good at motivating staff seek advice, and perhaps employ people who are

STAFF CHURN/TURNOVER

If you have a high rate of staff churn/turnover you may have a problem. The key question is what churn rate is reasonable for your business and when should you begin to worry? Interestingly, some churn is generally considered to be a good thing. This is because if there is no new blood introduced into the company you may find that people and ideas stagnate, and the business starts to do less well than its competitors.

On the other hand, a high staff churn rate is very expensive in terms of time and money in recruiting and training new staff. Further, word may get around your business community that lots of people are leaving your company, which may reduce your standing as a good employer. All of this can lead to a dangerous downwards spiral, potentially making it increasingly difficult for you to recruit good people.

An analysis of 'The Sunday Times 100 best companies to work for' created by Best Companies Ltd indicates that the average staff churn is 16% (for this select band of companies), which might be considered surprisingly high.

The relationship between staff churn and various factors such as the success of the company is not a simple one. Interestingly, a few of the very best companies to work for have a higher than average churn rate, although it is not particularly clear why this should be. Others, which are clearly very successful in their fields, have churn rates of as low as 1 to 2%. However, there are other companies with high employee satisfaction and low staff churn rates, yet they have been less than successful. This is because there are some basic success factors which have to be met before employee satisfaction and low staff churn rates become significant factors in the prosperity of any company.

TOP TIPS

- Don't worry about staff churn too early on in the beginning of the company – it may well be necessary to have such turnover in order to end up with the right people, so as to develop the culture you want

- You can be successful with staff churns within a very wide range, however anything over 20% might justify some attention, and over 30% there is almost certainly a problem

- Some experts suggest that a churn of 5% or less is unhealthy in that little new blood is being introduced into the company. You need to be your own judge on this point

MORALE AND MOTIVATION

Many people think morale can be improved by throwing money at people, but this is not necessarily the case. Moreover, many managers see staff as a cost rather than an investment. It is an increasingly held view that:

> **"**Companies that view their staff as an investment generally fare better than those that see them purely as a cost. **"**

All but the smallest of companies need staff, hence the mantra *'no staff – no revenues – no company'* applies. It therefore makes good business sense to look after your staff by ensuring good morale which generally helps maximize motivation and results in staff being happy to be at work and so more productive.

If you ask some managers what motivates their staff they may say:

- ▶ good salary
- ▶ high job security
- ▶ opportunities for promotion.

Whereas the staff may say they are motivated by:

- ▶ being appreciated and respected
- ▶ having an understanding boss (or bosses)
- ▶ feeling involved and that they are being kept informed on what is going on within the company
- ▶ believing their ideas and inputs are welcomed and appreciated.

In this example it is clear that the manager's view is the complete opposite of the staff's. Be aware however that this is a generalization, that all people are different, and different people have different motivators. To get the very best out of every employee you need to understand what inspires them individually – a painstaking task, but the rewards can be immense. Indicators of poor morale include:

- ▶ poor timekeeping
- ▶ gloominess and pessimism

▶ unresponsiveness and poor communication

▶ high staff churn, i.e. well above the industry norm (>20% is bad)

▶ poor productivity

▶ high level of sick leave and absenteeism.

Techniques for improving morale include:

1 Management to be approachable

▶ an open door policy can be a chore but it helps morale tremendously.

2 Management to be seen

▶ take walkabouts at least once a week if not once per day

▶ let your staff see you and know who you are

▶ consider open plan offices

▶ take lunch in the staff restaurant or snack area whenever possible (if you have such a thing).

3 Regular communications

▶ try weekly Monday morning 'prayer' meetings with immediate reports, and have them carried throughout the company at all levels. Ensure that your juniors are allowed to have their say – it is a two-way communication process that is important, not just one way from the top down

▶ have regular monthly or quarterly meetings where the boss presents an update on the business and other company news to all staff

▶ talk to staff at all levels and at every opportunity – in the lift, the snack bar, passing in the corridor, etc.

▶ if you have a suggestions box, any suggestion which is not anonymous should receive feedback one way or another, so that the writer knows whether their idea had any merit, etc., and if not, why not

▶ align staff goals and ambitions with those of the company. Companies that align their goals with those of the staff are generally much more successful than those that do not bother. Of course it is important that the company's goals and mission are clear and readily understood, and then communicated to all the staff. It is advisable during these two-way communication sessions to determine what it is that really motivates your staff. Once you know the answer then you can work out a means for encouraging this self-motivation.

4   Training

Ensure there is a training programme in place for all staff. Training can be very expensive, but for smaller companies there are still cost-effective training programmes run by Business Link and the Enterprise Agencies, which can cost as little as £50 per course. To keep the cost down you do not have to send everyone in the same 12-month period, you can stagger attendance over a few years. But make sure everyone thinks they are getting their fair share. Ensure that when training is recommended in an appraisal, it is actually followed up and provided within the year, i.e. before the next appraiseal.

Do not forget that training can be as simple as an in-house presentation to staff about the company's products, how they are used, who the customers are, something about the market, etc. This can be run by a product marketing manager or similar person at negligible cost, but will enhance morale no end. It is amazing how many receptionists, secretaries, cleaners, etc., do not have the faintest idea as to what their company actually does!

5   Fair pay scales

It is essential that staff feel they are not being unfairly treated in terms of salary. Although pay is generally not openly discussed amongst employees, it is astonishing how information about people's salaries spreads through the grapevine. You need to ensure that you have pay-scales for each staff grade, and that you have a procedure for ensuring staff start in the right grade, at an appropriate salary level, and can progress appropriately. Obviously things like experience and qualifications come into play here, as do market forces, but every endeavour should be made to ensure fair pay. For this reason it is a good idea for salaries to be reviewed by a senior manager each year to ensure there is no great disparity in pay between staff at similar levels, doing similar work, both within any given department, and between different departments.

6   Incentivization

Bonuses can be an incentive. There are broadly two types, personal and company wide. The former relates to the personal performance of an individual. Salespeople, for instance, are invariably incentivized by bonuses based on sales/revenue achieved. Company performance schemes are based on the performance of the company as a whole. While a company-wide scheme is very attractive to employees it does not guarantee good morale *per se*. It is seen as an attractive perk when the company is recruiting, however.

There is a view that for some jobs, incentivization does not work in the long term, and does not bring about lasting productivity improvements.

Given such a minefield it may be appropriate to seek specialist advice before proceeding with any particular system.

7   Recognition

People like to have their efforts/achievements recognized. This can be by pay and/or bonus, but publicizing an employee's achievement ensures their work colleagues get to know that they have done well, and increases their self-esteem no end. Such a scheme also often fosters a competitive spirit between employees, which can be good for productivity. You do need to be careful that the arrangement does not backfire, however; sometimes, in certain settings, those that do well can be seen as pandering to management and ill feeling can arise as a result, so care is needed in the implementation and ongoing monitoring of such a scheme.

8   Responsibility

People much prefer a carrot to a stick. Most people are capable of taking on far more responsibility than their job normally requires and generally respond positively to being given a relatively free reign (where this is possible within the confines of the specific work setting) to achieve high-level goals. Often staff find new and more productive ways of doing things when left to their own devices, and feel they have more control over their work environment – leading to greater morale and motivation.

Moreover, people work better in an environment where there is not a blame culture, and where mistakes can be made without fear of recrimination. Of course it is important to ensure that lessons are learnt from any errors, and are not repeated or made maliciously. When there is no fear of blame staff start to enjoy their work and begin to be ever more productive as a team.

A final point

Remember that companies with more than one member of staff need their employees in order to carry out their business. Those people are human beings with, e.g. partners, families, mortgages and other financial millstones around them, etc. Their goals in life, much like yours, are to be happy, healthy, and to survive economically; of course your additional goal as an entrepreneur will be to be successful in business as well. Always remember that your staff are human and treat them in a way that they will appreciate and in a way that you yourself would wish to be treated.

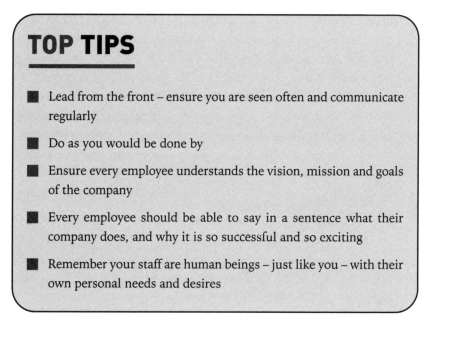

TOP **TIPS**

- Lead from the front – ensure you are seen often and communicate regularly

- Do as you would be done by

- Ensure every employee understands the vision, mission and goals of the company

- Every employee should be able to say in a sentence what their company does, and why it is so successful and so exciting

- Remember your staff are human beings – just like you – with their own personal needs and desires

HR PROCESSES AND PROCEDURES

For sole traders you hardly need HR processes and procedures but, for any business employing staff, there will be a need for certain minimum documentation, for instance employment contracts and job descriptions for all staff. Other more formal HR processes and procedures, including an HR manual, should be introduced as soon as practicable. There is no magic size at which you should introduce such formalities, but you would be well advised to start considering such things whenever you start to employ staff.

While small firms might be aghast at the thought of such bureaucracy, you need to be aware that it is almost guaranteed that a lack of defined HR processes and procedures will come back to haunt you, and/or the company, before very long.

The reason I say this is that employment law is a hot topic, both in the UK and in a European context. The number of new employment laws and regulations seems to be growing exponentially, and it is difficult even for large companies with large HR departments to keep pace, let alone small businesses.

All companies must abide by the law and so if you have an issue with an employee without the necessary processes and procedures in place, the company will be on the back foot should there be any litigation.

The following documentation should be available in any company with employees:

1   HR manual

The manual should state all the processes and procedures relating to staff matters and include *inter alia*:

- working hours
- overtime arrangements
- holiday entitlement, pay and notice
- maternity/paternity arrangements
- notice periods
- salary payment arrangements

> eligible expenses and how to claim them

> pay in lieu of notice

> location of employment

> grievance procedures.

2   Contract of employment for each employee

This will include many of the headings covered in the company HR manual but with specific reference to the employee to whom it applies, i.e. it will also include salary details , benefits, etc.

3   Job description for each employee

Fortunately pro forma HR documentation is fairly readily available. You could of course obtain such documentation from an employment lawyer; you could hire an HR consultant to put everything in place for you; the UK personnel organization (the Chartered Institute of Personnel and Development (CIPD)) can also advise; and lastly you could purchase standard pro forma HR documentation on the internet.

TOP TIPS

■ Make sure all staff have up-to-date employment contracts and job descriptions

■ Make sure the company has an up-to-date employee (HR) manual, which includes grievance procedures, etc.

■ Ensure all staff know of its existence and have access to it, or even have their own copy

EMPLOYEE LEGAL DISPUTES

It should be understood that there is now a proliferation of laws relating to employee rights, ranging from discrimination (sex, age, race, religion) and working time directives to maternity/paternity rights, etc. (These are all quite involved and space does not permit full treatment of them here.) In addition, every employee has a right to an employment contract and a job description which must be supplied within three months of joining the company, and there should be an employee handbook available giving all the relevant employee terms and conditions, processes and procedures. Failure to have provided these documents, and for them not to have covered the requisite issues should a court case arise, could result in a disastrous outcome for your business, since it will probably not have a leg to stand on.

Unfortunately, if you fall foul of the law and are taken to court, you may end up:

- ▶ paying large fees for lawyers
- ▶ having to pay a fine, which in some instances can be as much as £50,000
- ▶ having to devote considerable managerial time and effort to present your version of events and
- ▶ whatever the outcome you can find your business suffers from bad publicity.

Accordingly it is worth doing things by the book and, in any case, ignorance of the law is not regarded as any excuse. For many small companies, and especially start-ups, being taken to court can be the last straw, so attention to these details is well worth the effort. It need not be expensive to implement the processes and procedures, since some low-cost sources of advice do exist.

There are a few principles which are well worth following:

- ▶ appoint a good HR manager/director as soon as the company grows to a sufficient size that you can justify and fund such a resource
- ▶ obtain legal/professional advice regarding employment contracts, etc.
- ▶ establish an HR manual with requisite processes and procedures, etc.

If you find yourself in trouble, or just need some basic HR advice, the Institute of Directors offers free advice to members, which can be very useful and cost effective (see Appendix 5 for details).

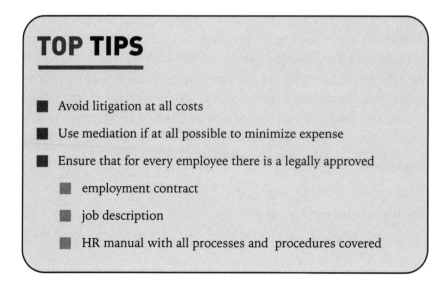

EMPLOYER LEGAL RESPONSIBILITIES

Employers have certain key responsibilities for their employees under various legislative acts. The most important include the following:

- ▶ to provide a contract of employment, job description and have available an HR handbook
- ▶ to ensure a safe working environment
- ▶ to not discriminate on the grounds of race, sex, age or religion
- ▶ to pay fair wages and not to pay below the minimum wage
- ▶ to not require employees to work more than 40 hours per work without their agreement
- ▶ to provide a minimum of 20 days' holiday a year excluding bank holidays.

Note that these requirements may change with time; you would be well advised to keep up to date on these minimum requirements (see Appendix 5).

TOP **TIPS**

■ Do not ignore these basic legal requirements

COMPANY SECURITY AND STAFF

The world is becoming an ever more competitive place, and more and more businesses are beginning to realize that their company's know-how (which can range from intellectual property and designs to pricing strategies, etc.) is of potential value to competitors.

Unscrupulous competitors can often use quite sophisticated techniques to obtain information about your company, many of which are related to your staff. Examples include:

▶ Industrial spies targeting staff to gain inside information by, for instance, frequenting the local pubs where your staff congregate and striking up conversations.

▶ Lax or no use of passwords on computers – which can leave the company open to attack. Simple passwords can easily be detected using dictionary attacks so the best passwords involve strings of a minimum of eight letters and numerals which have no particular meaning.

▶ Some competitors have been known to plant their staff with the targeted company as employees to ascertain secrets.

▶ Ensure adequate financial controls – for example, always have two staff members sign a cheque.

▶ Ensure staff do not leave laptops unattended and take every measure to avoid them being stolen.

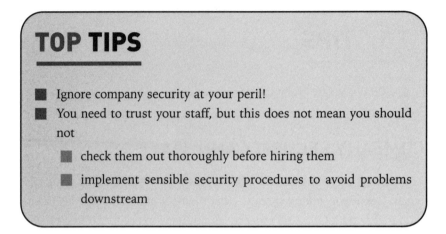

TOP TIPS

- Ignore company security at your peril!
- You need to trust your staff, but this does not mean you should not
    - check them out thoroughly before hiring them
    - implement sensible security procedures to avoid problems downstream

6

Sales and marketing

SALES AND MARKETING EMERGENCY PACK

Some sales and product problems which are commonly experienced by businesses are given in Table 6.1.

Table 6.1 Some sales/product warning signs, possible causes and possible solutions

Warning sign	Possible causes	Possible solutions
Increase in number of returns (faulty goods, etc)	Poor production/design quality	Review product design and manufacture
Price erosion	Product may have lost its appeal hence can only be sold at reduced prices (means reduced margins) Increased competition	Review pricing in market-place especially competitors' products and pricing strategies
Losing customers	Prices too high Product obsolete Inadequate sales and marketing activity	Speak to customers and find out truth
Repeat business declining	Product design needs improvment Weakness in sales and marketing organization	Speak to customers Review product marketing, sales and marketing organization and activity,

Table 6.1 continued

Warning sign	Possible causes	Possible solutions
	New competitors Existing competitors become more innovative	Review competitor activity
Fewer customers coming through the door	Poor advertising, etc, and marketing generally Poor products	Determine reasons, speak to old customers, review sales and product issues
Increase in number of complaints	Potential for reduced sales and hence lower revenues	Determine the cause(s) of the complaint and address it/them
Product release delays	Longer than planned R&D Production problems Approval/standards delays	Understand issues and reschedule/apply more resources, etc.

MARKETING

Marketing is all about setting the scene so that your customers are aware of your business and will willingly buy from you at prices which are mutually acceptable, such that you achieve your targeted sales levels. It covers such things as making sure that:

▶ the product is what customers want

▶ customers are aware that the product exists

▶ customers are aware they can obtain the product/service from you

▶ customers appreciate why your product is so attractive, such a good buy and better than the competition's

▶ customers know where, and how, they can physically buy your product/service.

It is absolutely essential that you understand what it is your customers want (i.e. product features), that they are prepared to buy it, how much they might pay for it, when they want it, the quality level desired, and any post-sales support expected.

Marketing is a topic that is often little understood, yet is key to the success of a business. It is not the intention of this book to provide a full treatise on the subject of marketing, however it is helpful for the reader to be aware of the following points.

Consumer behaviour

This is all about understanding your customers, be they other businesses or consumers. In particular it is about understanding their needs and how best they might be addressed by you, the potential supplier.

Be aware that customers are very good at changing their minds; they may wish to alter their technical requirements – sometimes at the last moment, or delay the purchase for a myriad of reasons, or suggest you reduce your prices to still get their order.

Market research

Very often, and especially for consumer markets, it is necessary to carry out market research in order to better understand the market size, the market requirements, the prospects of customers buying from your business, etc. This can be very expensive using specialist market research companies, but it can also be performed, in appropriate circumstances, comparatively cheaply by sending out your own questionnaires.

Product policy and planning

As a start-up or young business you are most likely to be focused on one or a small range of, products or services, or one particular market sector. You could in theory provide a large assortment of products and services, but this would probably not make economic sense in most cases. In practice, most businesses focus on a particular sector, or even a niche, and provide products and services within it. In this way the business can benefit from a more economic method of working.

Where your business does offer a range of products or services, this is known as the 'marketing mix'. You can have a divergent range of products and services, which all meet a particular customer requirement; or alternatively you can have a convergent product range, which means focusing on a few mainstream and highly profitable products or services.

When introducing new products or services there are many factors to consider, including the additional costs, risks, impact on staffing and bottom line returns, including time to break even.

Financial considerations include such things as opportunity cost and incremental costs.

Product timing is also a crucial issue. Critical examples of where timing of the introduction of a product to the market can have dire consequences for a business are given below:

1   **Moving markets**

The timing of the introduction of a new product is crucial. So many companies in recent times, especially high-tech ones, have developed the world's best gizmo, with no perceived competition, guaranteed to dramatically reduce customers' operating costs, etc. Financing is found readily, not least because the customers say they want the product. Everything looks rosy for a while – until the customers find that their strategies have not been working, that for example they have overspent on acquisitions, buying licences, the stock market crashes, they are heavily burdened with debt, etc. (An excellent example is the telecoms boom and bust era of the late 1990s and early 2000s.) In such circumstances what do these customers do? They stop all capital expenditure, which means they put a hold on buying your new gizmo. Not only that, but the market develops into a permanently depressed state, to the point where there is no prospect of any purchases of the new gizmo for maybe as much as five years.

In these circumstances cashflow control by the gizmo developer is critical; but the cash in hand will only last for a limited time, and if there are no other sources of revenue then the company can only survive so long. The company's investors may feel it is worth investing further to keep it afloat until the customers start purchasing again. However there are numerous instances where the plug has been pulled and the company has had to close down, through no fault of its own, just because the customers changed their minds.

2   **Being too early**

A very common problem for start-ups, and especially technology start-ups, is developing a technology and/or product but then finding that there is no market for it – at least for the time being.

It may indeed be the most wonderful widget product in the world, but if the customers do not wish to buy it, for whatever reason, then the company has a major problem.

Reasons why customers may not wish to buy your widget might include:

- they perceive buying from your company as being too risky, since you are a start-up and may not be around to support the product in years to come
- they may be strapped for cash and restricting their spending for the time being
- they may not understand the benefits of the product
- the product may be too advanced for there to be any national or international standards and they would prefer to wait until such standards are developed and published.

3 Being too late

Eventually even when a new idea is developed by a start-up or small company, larger companies eventually get themselves into gear and, if they perceive a big enough market, they will move to address it. Unfortunately large companies are like oil tankers, once they are on the move they become difficult to stop. Hence the big companies use their power in the marketplace to convince customers to buy from them. Once these industry giants are motivated it is very difficult for you, as a new entrant, to break into the market – unless perhaps you have a significant differentiator, which offers major financial or other advantages to the customers.

Remember that the existing players may well be milking the market (i.e. cash-cow phase, and might be in a position to drop their prices to knock you out of play, without affecting their own profitability significantly).

TOP TIPS

■ Always keep an eye on the market – it never stands still and while customers might be keen to buy one year they may not be in 12 months' time

■ Being too early with a product can be as bad as being too late

■ Ensure your business plan includes a sensitivity analysis to show the effect of moving markets

Pricing

Getting pricing right is absolutely crucial. Charge too much and you will not sell too many of your products, conversely charging too little may mean you sell a large number of products, but your profit margin may be minimal, or non-existent (see also p. 55).

Advertising and promotion

There are a number of techniques for promoting your products and services, namely:

1   Get your customers to do the work for you! Word of mouth is the most powerful form of marketing, so encourage your customers to recommend you to other people. You could consider incentivizing them by offering them a discount on their next purchase, or a free product or service, for every successful introduction.

    Bear in mind that it is also much more cost-effective to keep an existing customer than to find a new one, so the message has to be to make sure you look after your existing customers, and understand their changing needs (before the competition!).

2   Advertising

    There are many forms of advertising including:

- hoardings
- television and radio
- newspapers and magazines
- internet.

One of the problems with large-scale advertising is that it may not be focused and might be rather expensive. For smaller businesses there are nevertheless numerous local, reasonably cost-effective advertising opportunities, which can be quite economic. Examples include:

- adverts in local newspapers and magazines
- flyers.

You can spend a fortune on advertising and get no increase in business. It is therefore absolutely essential that any advertising campaign is targeted and its effectiveness monitored.

Internet advertising on a 'pay per click' basis can be a very cost-effective means of advertising and has the benefit that you can monitor and control the costs quite well. As the internet becomes more and more popular for online purchases this approach is likely to be ever more widely used. Viral marketing is another internet technique whereby the fame of some interesting/unique feature of your website, or whatever, is spread in a 'viral' manner via e-mails, chat rooms, etc.

There are also some effective ways of advertising at little or no cost. For instance, if your business does something newsworthy you might find that your company name is splashed all over your local newspaper – hopefully for all the right reasons! You may have to jog the editor a little by sending a press release. Another option is what are called advertorials, where the newspaper does a write-up on your company, as if it was a regular newspaper item, the usual caveat being that you have to pay for a little bit of advertising; this can nevertheless be a very cost-effective way of getting you company name known locally.

3   Exhibitions, etc.

Big exhibitions can be expensive to participate in for the smaller business, but there are local events which are much more economic and affordable. You do need to do your homework in advance to determine how worthwhile participation in such exhibitions might be however.

Moreover, if you do participate, you do need a mechanism for taking visitors' details, so that if they appear to be a true potential customer, you can follow up after the event.

4   Networking

You should never forget the benefits of networking, especially if you are in the services sector. Networking involves attending events where you can meet potential customers. The Institute of Directors, and Chambers of Commerce, to name but two organizations, often arrange 'networking breakfasts' or 'networking evenings' where you can meet other businesspeople, many of whom might be interested in your products or services (see Appendix 5 for contacts).

5   E-mail newsletters

This is a fairly recent phenomenon, but one which can be remarkably effective. Newsletters are typically an update on developments in the your industry, and can also include outcomes of surveys – basically anything that will interest the recipient sufficiently that they will open the newsletter, read it, and become familiar with your company name, and your products and services.

Distribution channels

Marketing includes choices about how to distribute your product or service. There are many options and they will vary according to your type of business, and any decisions you make about how to get your product/service to market. They will include:

Direct:

▶   internet
▶   own sales channels, i.e. business-to-business (B2B) marketing
▶   own shop(s).

Indirect:

▶   shops not owned by you
  ▶   small retail
  ▶   department stores

- ▶ chain stores
- ▶ discount stores
- ▶ wholesalers
- ▶ franchising.

International marketing

Marketing abroad can be highly challenging, and you need to know what you are doing. Having said this even small businesses can achieve great things by selling and marketing internationally.

The UK Department of Trade and Industry (DTI) and Business Link can both provide valuable information about trading abroad (see references in Appendix 5).

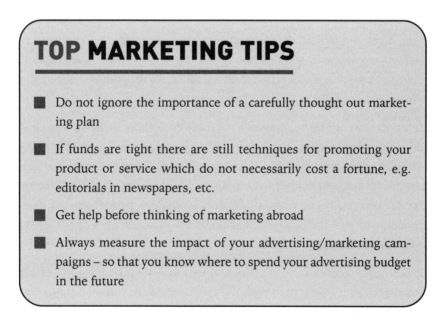

TOP MARKETING TIPS

- ■ Do not ignore the importance of a carefully thought out marketing plan

- ■ If funds are tight there are still techniques for promoting your product or service which do not necessarily cost a fortune, e.g. editorials in newspapers, etc.

- ■ Get help before thinking of marketing abroad

- ■ Always measure the impact of your advertising/marketing campaigns – so that you know where to spend your advertising budget in the future

SALES

Sales is all about relating to your customers and closing a sale/deal. It follows therefore that the way you treat your customers is absolutely crucial to the long-term success of your business. It is an obvious fact that if there are no customers you have no business!

In the case of a start-up your business plan will make assumptions about when the first customers will start placing orders with you, and at what rate the number of customers, and the size of their orders, will grow. In the case of existing companies looking to grow, it is the increase in the number of customers, and the amount they spend with you each year, which are critical.

Anyone such as a VC or bank manager, reviewing your business plan will home in on your customer and revenue projections. It is a common problem with such forecasts that they are invariably too optimistic in terms of

▶ when the first customers will place their orders

▶ the size of their orders, and

▶ the rate at which the customer base grows.

It is therefore essential that your business plan includes a sensitivity analysis with a pessimistic scenario taking account of these factors, so that both you, and your shareholders and funders, can make realistic assessments on the viability and likely success of your venture.

It is not unknown for businesses to be the hottest thing in their sector, with potential customers all lined up ready to buy the products, and then an external event results in those customers deciding not to buy in the foreseeable future. This was a not uncommon phenomenon when the telecoms sector went from boom to bust in the 2000/2002 period, leaving many start-ups to face the prospect of winding up prematurely without having sold any products.

It is worth mentioning at this juncture that it is not always easy to obtain customers: they do not automatically come flocking to your door, and it can be quite time-consuming and expensive to obtain them, even though you might have a wonderful product. But once you have found them it is absolutely crucial that you retain them, hence they must be made to feel that they are totally wanted by you, and that nothing is too much trouble. This is because the cost of finding new customers is generally considerably more than retaining existing ones.

However, given the adage that 'the customer is king', and the fact that you have no business without customers, the importance of having good people – who one way or another bring in those customers and the accompanying revenues – cannot be underestimated. Indeed the best salespeople are absolutely worth their weight in gold!!!

One of the most important messages about sales is *'listen to your customer'*. If you develop a rapport with your customers, more often than not they will tell you what they want, when they want it, and even how you might best provide it, and at what price. This is invaluable customer feedback, yet all too often the customer is heard but the messages are not taken on board. Not listening to your customer in this way is unforgivable, since many companies pay market intelligence companies a fortune for this type of information. Of course you should not necessarily accept everything that the customer tells you, but at least you have a good starting point from which to negotiate something which the customer might be happy with, and which is sensible for you to supply. This comment applies to pricing and delivery as much as to the product specification itself.

Of course, it is customers who generate the sales revenues, and there are some golden rules to follow:

▶ understand your customer and their needs
▶ be close to them at all times
▶ agree mutually acceptable payment terms
▶ agree a price which generates a profit (unless there is a very good reason for not doing so, like longer-term prospects)
▶ do not be reliant on any one customer
▶ recognize that customers (even big ones) can go bust.

If you are large enough to warrant your own dedicated salesperson (or team), then these people could be worth their weight in gold – if they bring in sufficient business. Recruiting the very best salespeople is not always that easy, however. Salespeople, by their very nature, tend to be outgoing and persuasive, and as a consequence they will probably be good at selling themselves, but it does not always follow that they will be good at selling your product/service. You would be well advised to thoroughly check their past performance before hiring them and if you do find someone good then hire them and reward them well. Salespeople are invariably paid a base salary, plus commission based on the level of sales they achieve – so as to motivate them adequately. Make sure you allow for the commission costs in your business plan.

Problems related to sales quite often fall into one of two areas:

1 Sales too low

Obviously sales levels which are below your forecast levels, mean that your revenues will be less than planned, with the potential that, if your costs are not reduced sufficiently, your bottom line profits will be severely impacted.

Close, regular monitoring of sales should flag up any prospective problems early on, while there is still a chance to address any adverse situation – before it becomes critical.

Some options which might be considered – given poor sales – might include:

▶ deploying additional sales staff

▶ training or otherwise improving the closing abilities of your sales staff

▶ addressing any areas of weakness preventing customers from placing orders with you

▶ offering discounts or incentives

▶ considering any competitive action and adopt a counter strategy

▶ adapting/improving your marketing.

2 Sales more than planned

'How can this be a problem?' I hear you ask. Surely sales greater than forecast has to be a good thing? Sometimes they are indeed a good thing and the business can handle the extra workload but, ironically, too many sales can also sometimes be a problem. For instance, if you are unable to meet the increased demand (due perhaps to limited production capacity) your customers may desert you in the future, and in extreme cases they may sue you if you are in legal default (depending on the terms of any contract).

You may need to increase your operations to meet the greater demand, by bolstering production capacity and staffing for instance, which may present difficulties in respect of cashflow, staff recruitment, etc., and could, depending on the economics, actually cause you to make less profit than if your sales were at a reduced level.

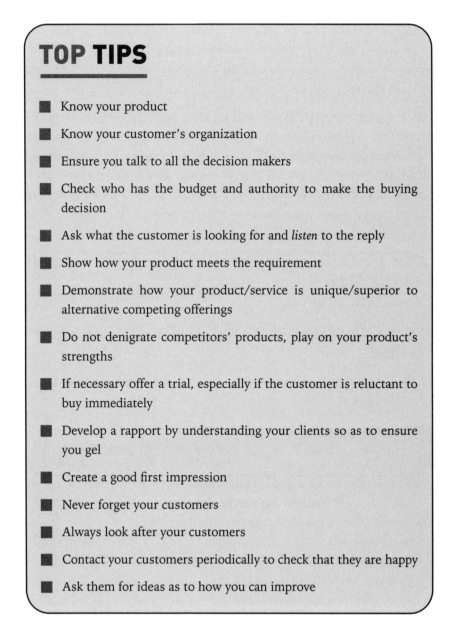

TOP **TIPS**

- Know your product
- Know your customer's organization
- Ensure you talk to all the decision makers
- Check who has the budget and authority to make the buying decision
- Ask what the customer is looking for and *listen* to the reply
- Show how your product meets the requirement
- Demonstrate how your product/service is unique/superior to alternative competing offerings
- Do not denigrate competitors' products, play on your product's strengths
- If necessary offer a trial, especially if the customer is reluctant to buy immediately
- Develop a rapport by understanding your clients so as to ensure you gel
- Create a good first impression
- Never forget your customers
- Always look after your customers
- Contact your customers periodically to check that they are happy
- Ask them for ideas as to how you can improve

BUSINESS DEVELOPMENT

Business development is subtly different from sales. It is the process which occurs before any sales can be made and involves identifying a project (for which you might bid for instance), identifying the customer, developing a close relationship, understanding the customer's requirements, developing a strategy for meeting the customer requirements, appraising your own organization of the upcoming customer requirements (i.e. the product specification, etc.), and ensuring your company is on the customer's radar and list of prospective bidders, etc.

At an appropriate time, which can vary from project to project, from customer to customer, and from firm to firm, there is a handover from the business development activity to the sales team. Sometimes, for continuity, the business development team may work hand in hand with the sales team to ensure success. There is nothing written in stone, the ultimate goal being the successful award of a contract to your company.

TOP TIPS

■ Know your customers and their requirements both now and in the future

■ Ensure you feed back your findings to the people that need to know within your company

■ Ensure your customer knows that you can meet their requirements – perhaps better than any of your competitors

7

Legal matters

GENERAL

Lawyers can prove to be indispensable, and should be used whenever appropriate. However, you can obtain plenty of useful legal information from the internet, by just typing key words into a search engine. Other free advice is provided by business support member-based organizations such as the Institute of Directors (IoD), and the Federation of Small Businesses, etc. (see Appendix 5 for website references). These and various other professional bodies provide a limited amount of free legal advice to members each year.

Litigation (legal disputes) of whatever sort can be expensive, and it is therefore always a good principle to do whatever you can to avoid such situations, for instance, try to settle a dispute amicably whenever possible.

COMPANY LEGAL ENTITIES

When setting up your business you need to decide what legal entity to adopt for your business (if any). The principal choices are:

limited liability company (Ltd)

Such companies have their liability limited to the shareholders' stakes, and are entitled to put 'Limited' or 'Ltd' after their company names. There must be at least one member/shareholder/director plus a company secretary. A limited liability company cannot sell its shares to the public.

Public limited company (Plc)

The public liability of a Plc is limited to the shareholders' combined stakes, but a minimum of two members/shareholders/directors are required, together with a company secretary. In this instance shares can be sold to the public and indeed there must be £50,000 of issued shares before the company can trade.

Partnership

With a partnership the partners are in effect the shareholders and are responsible jointly for all the debts of the partnership. Partners are usually regarded as being self-employed, and pay taxes accordingly. A partnership agreement is drawn up between the partners.

Limited liability partnership (Llp)

This is similar to a partnership except that the partners' liability is limited, as defined in the Llp agreement, and is usually the partners' combined stake in the partnership.

Llps can be arranged so that the partners are self-employed, as with normal partnerships or, if the necessary arrangements are put in place, the partners can be employees and pay tax accordingly, and the Llp also pays taxes rather like a limited liability company, including corporation taxes.

Sole trader

This is not a legal entity as such, but is included here so that all the options can be noted. In the case of a sole trader, who is the proprietor, all liabilities rest personally with the sole trader, who is deemed to be self-employed for tax purposes.

If in doubt as to which option is best for you, you should seek professional advice from an accountant and/or lawyer.

TOP TIPS

■ Professional advice should be sought before deciding on any particular legal entity, since the implications – both legally and financially – will vary significantly from case to case.

FINDING A LAWYER

It is usually best to use a lawyer who has been recommended, is within easy reach, and who has genuine practical experience of the field in which you need advice, and to whom you feel you can relate. For normal legal business there is almost certainly a lawyer in your locality who will be able to meet your normal requirements.

It is possible to get your business underway without the help of a lawyer. However. if you are looking to obtain external funding then it is almost certain that you will need their services. If you are a smallish start-up looking to raise funds from family, your local bank or business angels, the legal aspects can be relatively straightforward and not too costly, although you will have to cover any legal costs yourself.

If you are a start-up with grand plans and looking to raise considerable funding from VCs, i.e. more than £1M, the legal costs could be quite considerable. In such circumstances you may wish to find a law firm which is prepared to share some risk regarding the legal costs. The reason for this is that while you are sure your grand plan will obtain funding and the world is your oyster, in practice there are many pitfalls which can bring the venture to a standstill, while still having incurred not insignificant legal costs.

It is therefore to your advantage to find a law firm which is prepared to work on a success-based fee arrangement. The slight downside (for you) is that the law firm may want more advantageous terms (for them) in the event of a successful outcome. Also worth checking out (assuming it is a road you are happy to go down) is whether you would like the idea of having the legal fees split between cash and a stake in your business, maybe on a 50:50 basis.

The important thing is that these real world aspects are recognized from the start and that a suitable, mutually acceptable agreement on terms is agreed at the outset. Put another way, do not be afraid to ask the question, 'Who bears the legal costs if the fundraising deal does not go through?'

There are many would-be entrepreneurs whose plans have soured because they employed a law firm which undertook considerable work but funding did not materialize, or some other gremlin appeared, such that the project could not proceed, and the founders ended up having to pay the firm, without having achieved their goal of creating a new company.

TOP TIPS

- Finding a good lawyer is like finding a good plumber – go on personal recommendation wherever possible
- Agree terms right at the outset
- Understand the implications for legal costs if the project does not proceed as planned

EU REGULATIONS

The EU continues to introduce new rules and regulations for businesses, but unfortunately ignorance of the law is not an excuse for non-compliance. The message therefore has to be do your homework; fortunately a great deal of research can be performed relatively inexpensively using the internet. If in doubt however consult a lawyer specializing in the appropriate field.

TOP **TIPS**

■ Obtain advice if you have any doubts about EU regulations

BEING A COMPANY DIRECTOR

It is up to the shareholders to appoint the directors who will run the company on their behalf. However, you cannot become a company director if:

1 you have been disqualified by a court from acting as a company director

2 you are an undischarged bankrupt

3 in Scotland if you are under the age of 16

4 over 70 years of age and in a plc or subsidiary thereof, unless specifically approved by a general meeting of the company.

TOP **TIPS**

■ Ensure you are doing things properly from the outset and seek advice if in any doubt

DIRECTOR'S RESPONSIBILITIES AND THE COMPANIES ACTS

Director's responsibilities are well defined in the Companies Act but in most instances it is easier to check out the various business websites, including that of the Institute of Directors (see Appendix 5 for website references and also Chapter 17 on corporate governance).

Director's responsibilities in summary include the following:

1   Every company director has a responsibility to ensure that statutory documents are delivered to Companies House as and when required. This includes accounts, annual returns, notice of change of directors or secretaries, or their particulars, and change of registered office.

2   Directors must:

> not have been disqualified by a court from being a director. If you have you need the court's permission to take such a position

> not be an undischarged bankrupt. If you are you need the court's permission to take such a position

> be over 16 years of age if based in Scotland

> be under 70 years of age if in a public limited company unless the appointment is approved by a general meeting of the company

> be appointed in accordance with the company's Articles of Association.

3   Non-executive directors have the same legal responsibilities as executive directors.

4   Directors must be appointed in accordance and comply with the company's legal documents, that is the Memorandum and Articles of Association, which define what directors can and cannot do.

5   Directors must exercise a degree of skill and care, and act as any reasonable person would in running the business.

6   Directors must act in good faith and in the interests of the company as a whole. This includes ensuring equality of treatment of all shareholders, declaring any conflicts of interest, and not making any personal profit at the company's expense.

7   Directors must obey the law which includes:

> submitting company accounts and returns to Companies House on time

> complying with

    – health and safety laws

    – employment law

    – tax law, including ensuring the payment of tax, VAT and National Insurance on time

> ▶ being responsible for the actions of employees in so far as they pertain to the company.

Acting improperly as a director can lead to fines, disqualification from being a director, personal liability for the company's debts, or even a criminal conviction.

The Institute of Directors has useful booklets on the subject of directors' responsibilities (free to members).

TOP **TIPS**

- Remind yourself of your responsibilities as a director from time to time

- Always submit your accounts and returns to Companies House on time

- Always pay income tax, National Insurance, corporation tax, and VAT on time

- Review your procedures periodically to ensure you still comply with employment, health and safety and other relevant laws

DECLARATION AND CONFLICT OF INTERESTS

You must at all times be sure as a director that nothing you are doing, or someone close to you is doing, or something which you (or someone close to you) owns, presents a conflict of interest with regard to your business.

An example may simply be that you have a shareholding in a competing business. If it is a shareholding in a public quoted company, and you have no other executive or non-executive role within that other company, then there is probably no problem. If, however, as a shareholder you held an executive, or indeed a non-executive director's position, then there would indeed be a conflict.

When such conflict of interest is apparent, then the next step is to declare it to the board and/or senior management. It is then up to senior management to determine how significant the conflict is in practice. Depending on the significance of the conflict the board may require that you give up whatever it is that is causing the conflict.

It is an area which can cause major difficulty for some people, but as a principle, it is always best to play safe and declare even the slightest perceived conflict of interest.

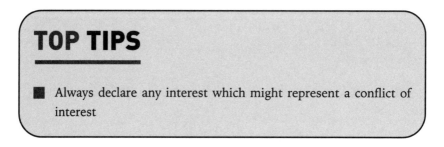

TOP TIPS

■ Always declare any interest which might represent a conflict of interest

CONNECTED PERSONS

This is a little bit like conflict of interest but applied to people, typically relatives, etc. For instance if your spouse works for a competitor then you are a connected person. Likewise if you employ your spouse in some capacity within your own business then they are connected.

Clearly in some instances the issue is trivial, in others it can be major and potentially significantly affect the future prospects of the business. As always, and especially if in any doubt, it is best to raise the connected persons issue with the board and see if a satisfactory way ahead can be determined. However, in extreme cases, it may mean that one or other person can no longer remain with the company. It is therefore not always an easy decision to be upfront on such matters, but honesty is definitely the best policy.

TOP TIPS

- Be honest about any connected persons. If you are not, the truth will surely come out eventually and result in somebody's downfall at some stage

DIRECTOR'S WARRANTIES

These are very important. Any funder who wishes to finance your venture will require the directors to warrant the validity of the business plan and any other information supplied to the funder, which might have helped influence them in their decision to fund your venture.

The warranty merely involves signing a sheet of paper in which you confirm the accuracy of the documentation which you have supplied.

However, if you have warranted some data and it is subsequently determined to be in error, then the funder can claim retribution, which can be extremely serious at a personal level. The penalties are typically stated in the legal documentation relating to the funding and a director may have to pay as much as three times their annual salary in the event that any submission knowingly contained incorrect, or even fraudulent, data.

TOP TIPS

- The moral here is that it is absolutely essential that the data included in a business plan is as accurate as possible and that, where there is any doubt about the accuracy of a piece of data, this should be openly stated as being a best guess or estimate

DIRECTOR'S INDEMNITY INSURANCE

Recognizing the minefield that company law presents, and the fact that being a limited company does not totally absolve directors of all their responsibilities in certain circumstances, it is recommended that all company directors take out director's indemnity insurance. Many companies automatically pay for all their directors to have this valuable cover. Typically the cost is £300–£500 p.a. and if bought personally the cost can be set against tax.

Of course sole traders cannot avail themselves of quite the same benefits as a limited liability company director, since for the sole trader the buck stops with them. Nevertheless it is still worthwhile obtaining as much insurance as possible to mitigate any future disasters.

TOP **TIPS**

■ As a company director ensure you have director's indemnity insurance

COMPANY LAW

This book is not able to address the myriad issues relating to company law, however all directors are assumed to have full knowledge of the law. Ignorance of the law is not an excuse for breaking it.

Obviously larger firms will either have an in-house lawyer or will have retained the services of a law firm. For the smaller business obtaining legal advice can be very expensive. Some steps which smaller firms might pursue to mitigate the situation are as follows:

▶ attend a course on the responsibilities of directors and/or company law (for instance those run by the Institute of Directors)

▶ join an organization such as the Institute of Directors which provides a certain amount of free legal advice in a year. Other bodies include your local Chamber of Commerce, and the Federation of Small Businesses.

TOP **TIPS**

■ Attend a course on company law
■ Join a body such as the Institute of Directors which will help keep you updated on company law issues

LEGAL AGREEMENTS

It is possible to set up a company without incurring any legal costs, by using one of the many company registration firms who provide company set-up services typically for £50–80. Such an approach uses 'off the shelf' Articles and Memorandum of Association.

However things start to get more complicated if you:

1   want to include specific requirements in the Articles or Memorandum which relate specifically to your company
2   wish to rent property
3   need complicated shareholder documentation
4   are obtaining funding from a body such as a venture capital fund
5   are applying for intellectual property rights.

In these circumstances you have little option but to use the services of a good lawyer (see p. 115). Make sure you are open with your selected lawyer, and communicate all your thinking; unless you do this they may not be able to help you as fully as might otherwise be the case. Always check the documents produced by your lawyer, since you are the one who has to sign them, and will therefore be legally liable. If there is anything which you do not understand in the documentation do not be afraid to query it with your lawyer.

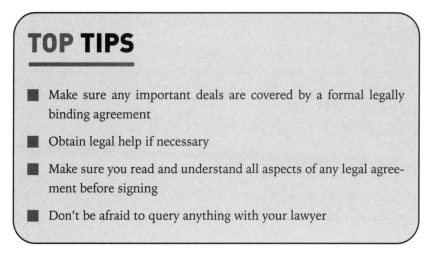

TOP TIPS

■ Make sure any important deals are covered by a formal legally binding agreement

■ Obtain legal help if necessary

■ Make sure you read and understand all aspects of any legal agreement before signing

■ Don't be afraid to query anything with your lawyer

PROPERTY LEASES

Entering into property agreements invariably commits you to long-term contracts and hence liabilities. Many businesses rent their accommodation and, being growing companies, often have to move fairly frequently to accommodate the extra staff, etc. However, property leases are not always ideal for small growing businesses, for the simple reason that landlords prefer long-term leases – for obvious reasons. Lease durations of five to ten years are not unusual, although lease terms of three years can sometimes be found and/or negotiated. Sometime the lease has a break at a mid-point, for instance a ten-year lease might have a break point at five years. This means that if you want the property for ten years it is yours, but that if you need to move out after just five years you can. Break points are always worth incorporating within a lease – if at all possible.

From your point of view signing a lease means you have a financial commitment for some years, which does not go away during the contracted term (except in particular circumstances which should be covered in the lease). Thus if your business falls on hard times the landlord will still expect their rent to be paid.

Always remember to try for a rent holiday when you are negotiating a lease. This is typically a period of up to three or so months, when your business will be settling in, fitting out etc., and may not be capable of producing any revenues. The kind landlord, recognizing such circumstances, might be prepared to grant you a short period during which you do not need to pay any rent. Always worth a try!

Renting can be problematical, especially if you are renting at a time of buoyant rental rates. It is not uncommon for leases to be signed at a high pound per square foot rate in a buoyant market and then, if the market deteriorates, competitors come in, renting at possibly a substantially lower rental rate, and you cannot do anything about it.

Many businesses fail due to having excessive rent commitments. Sometimes if you have a nice landlord you may be able to negotiate a rent holiday, or a period of reduced rent, but in the end they can bring about your demise if they do not get their money. Most landlords have little compunction in insisting on being paid what is due to them and if you don't pay up they would prefer to have a tenant who can afford the premises.

In some circumstances, if you cannot afford to pay the rent, you can move elsewhere and sublet the property, assuming this is permissible in your lease. At least this gets you off the hook, although if your subtenant defaults you are usually still liable for the rent to the landlord.

One solution for many young start-up companies is to use serviced offices, most of which do not require more than a month's notice. Also there are various business parks and 'incubation' centres for start-ups and smaller companies around the country, which do not normally require long leases. Your local Business Link can usually help advise you on their location (see Appendix 5).

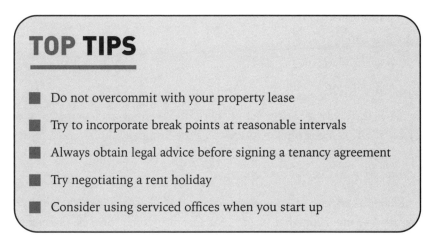

TOP **TIPS**

- ■ Do not overcommit with your property lease
- ■ Try to incorporate break points at reasonable intervals
- ■ Always obtain legal advice before signing a tenancy agreement
- ■ Try negotiating a rent holiday
- ■ Consider using serviced offices when you start up

THE BIBLE

When forming a company there are a number of legal documents which need to be produced. The basic ones are:

▶ Articles of Association

▶ Memorandum of Association

▶ Company House Registration document.

However there are potentially numerous other documents which might include:

▶ shareholder agreements

▶ service agreements (for directors)

▶ employment contracts for top team

▶ loan agreements

▶ any fixed charges (mortgages, etc.)

▶ investment agreements

▶ disclosure letters

▶ intellectual property information

▶ intellectual property assignments

▶ patent agreements

▶ know-how licence agreements

▶ consultancy agreements

▶ warrant instruments

▶ side letters

▶ powers of attorney

▶ copies of forms sent to Companies House.

It is usual to have a master set of these documents kept together in one place/file. This file is often referred to as the 'company Bible', and is often kept by the company secretary, the CFO, or the CEO, depending on the nature, style and size of the company.

The Bible is important because whenever there is some involvement in a transaction involving shares, etc., for instance some form of merger or acquisition, then the Bible will need to be reviewed by the board and inspected by all the various advisors.

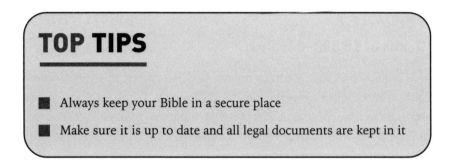

TOP TIPS

- Always keep your Bible in a secure place
- Make sure it is up to date and all legal documents are kept in it

GETTING MONEY FROM DEBTORS

General

Going to court to get money owed to you is only a last resort. Remember to try letters, culminating in a final warning letter to the effect that if payment is not made you will be referring the case to the small claims court. This sometimes results in the debt being paid. You can also use a solicitor to help you, and/or a debt recovery agent.

Small claims up to £5,000

For debts up to £5,000 you can use the small claims court system to recover the monies owed to you. You do need to have proof that the debt exists, so for your claim to be effective it helps to have the whole process fully documented with proof of supply, order invoice, chasing letters, etc.

The county court process requires that you complete a standard form (form N1 – obtainable from the Courts Service website – see Appendix 5), which includes details about the parties involved and the nature of the claim. A summons is then sent to the defendant who can either pay the monies owed, or pay part of the sum owed if they have some reasonable reason for so doing (e.g. only part of the goods have been supplied), or dispute the claim.

When a claim is disputed it goes to court where the evidence is heard by a judge, and a decision is usually made the same day. There is no formal appeals procedure. You have to pay the court fee upfront, but if you win the case the fees may be recovered from the debtor. If you lose you may be liable for costs.

Claims of £5,000–£15,000

This is known as the fast-track process and is pursued through a county court. It is usually a longer process than the small claims track and invariably goes to court. You are not expected to represent yourself, but this does mean solicitor's fees will be incurred, the costs of which might be recovered if judgment is in your favour.

Claims for £15,000–£50,000

This is referred to as the multi-track process for complex cases but is still heard in a county court. Otherwise as for the fast-track process.

High Court

The High Court, as opposed to a county court, can be used for very expensive and/or complex cases, however the legal costs are likely to be high.

Information on all these procedures can be seen on the Courts service website – see Appendix 5).

TOP TIPS

■ Try letters and final warnings first

■ Check out the best procedure for the size of debt

■ Obtain legal advice if felt necessary

PART TWO

Other topics

8

Strategic development issues

Some of the strategic development opportunities in this chapter may never be addressed by many start-ups. On the other hand, those that are planning to grow fast need to be aware of these opportunities and the associated issues which might arise. Remember also that business plans often need to cover a three to five year period, and some of these developmental opportunities may well occur within that timescale.

ACQUISITION

Acquisition of another company, be it competitor, supplier or customer, or indeed even another company outside your existing field of operation, can bring about immense advantages in terms of sales, customers, profitability, enhanced product range, etc.

It can also bring about the downfall of your company! All too often the perceived advantages of an acquisition are seen through rose-tinted glasses and in practice the problems turn out to be just too huge so that either part, or all, of your business fails.

Furthermore, people who would not dream of paying more than they have to in the local shops, often do not seem to worry about paying over the odds to acquire the company of their dreams. Remember that someone has to pay the bill, and paying too much may well mean it takes longer for the real financial benefits of the acquisition to come to fruition, and sometimes they are not seen at all – so be warned!

There is something about acquiring another company which acts as an elixir of power, boosting the egos of the acquiring team who often are all too convinced of its merits and ignore consideration of some of the downsides. Frequently any snags which are identified at the due diligence stage are seen as minor and readily addressable following completion of the deal. In practice things are never quite as they seem, despite the most thorough analysis. Cost reductions through economies of scale and the advantages of doing away with any duplication are often overestimated. The benefits in terms of increased sales may not materialize, and so on. The problems can be even worse if the acquired company is in a different country.

The moral is, therefore, as always when buying anything – 'buyer beware' (*caveat emptor*) – and make sure you really do understand the logic for the transaction and the likely outcomes. Make sure you do your sensitivity analyses, and assume some pessimistic outcomes, in order to get a really good handle on what the worst case scenarios might be.

Nothwithstanding these cautionary words it is possible to acquire companies and achieve a tremendously successful outcome, but invariably the acquiring company has really done its homework, really understands what it is buying, and has developed an appropriate strategy for bringing the two businesses together.

TOP **TIPS**

- ■ Do your homework thoroughly (due diligence)
- ■ Do not overpay if you can possibly avoid it, or unless you are sure about the financial merit of doing so

DIVERSIFICATION

Start-ups need to be careful about diversifying too early on in their development but, as they develop, the advantages will doubtless start to be considered. Growing companies often reach a stage in their development when they have saturated their market and need to look for other ways of increasing sales and profitability year on year. Diversification is one obvious answer.

Diversification can be achieved in a number of different ways, namely:

1   Geographical

You can look to expand into other regions within a country, or even consider other countries. Many companies have been very successful in this way, while others have had tremendous difficulties and in some cases experienced financial meltdown – as a result of underestimating the challenges and difficulties. Needless to say there are no guarantees, but it certainly does help if you do all your due diligence in detail, research the proposed markets, talk to local businesspeople, use the services of the UK DTI (Department of Trade and Industry (see website details in Appendix 5), and speak to the in-country commercial attaché at the embassy. Consider using the services of an agent or distributor. All of these things can only help to maximize your chances of success.

2   Product

You may have decided that the best way to diversify is to expand your product portfolio. This can often make a lot of sense and, where the new product is consistent with your existing product range, can utilize your existing manufacturing facilities. If you do not need new sales teams or different channels to market, etc., then this can be eminently sensible.

If, however, you are currently making cars, and you decide to manufacture soap, this may be a bridge too far! (This is obviously an extreme example but you can see the point.) Having said this, some businesses have been built up as conglomerates, with subsidiaries producing a broad range of products and services, and not necessarily in the same sector. Such conglomerates can be successful. However, analysis of such conglomerates often indicates that, with only a small number of exceptions, many eventually reach a point where they need to divest many of their non-core businesses and become a more focused operation.

3   Vertical integration

Vertical integration is when you integrate either a supplier or a customer into your business; this is in contrast to horizontal integration, which integrates competitors, or other operations in different sectors, but at the same level in the supply chain.

Once again it is not uncommon for senior managers to consider vertical integration as the way to expand. This can involve acquiring suppliers, channels to market, or even a customer.

Acquiring a supplier can often be seen to be very sensible, until it is realized they actually supply your competitors to, and that the latter are not so keen on being dependent on a company which is also owned by one of their competitors. You can appreciate that in such circumstances it would not be surprising to see sales in the supplier start to decline, with all the consequential problems. On the other hand there may be some significant strategic advantages to be had.

Acquiring channels to market, for instance sales outlets (e.g. shops), can be sensible but even here competitors who might have used those same outlets in the past may not wish to do so in the future, and hence revenues for those shops might fall following the acquisition.

TOP TIPS

■ If the proposed diversification appears too good to be true, it probably is

■ Recognize that the status quo before the diversification may not be maintained after the event

DIVESTMENT

Divestment as such is not normally an issue for start-ups, except that if a larger company is divesting itself of a non-core part of its business, and that business potentially complements your own in some way, then the possibility of considering an acquisition might not be unrealistic.

Divestment, or selling-off a business or part of a business, is very common. It often occurs when the company is having problems and decides it needs to downsize and/or divest itself of non-core activities. This can be good news in terms of, for instance, reducing the company's debt burden, but bad news for shareholders if the stock market analysts disagree with the strategy, and cause the share price to be reduced (this applies only to publicly quoted companies of course).

Another problematic outcome of a divestiture is if a competitor acquires the business and you still need the divested business's products. You might find prices or delivery times increasing, to your detriment.

TOP TIPS

■ Acquiring a divested business may be an attractive option – but make sure you do your homework

ORGANIC GROWTH

Organic growth is all about what you currently try to do, but in a bigger way. It can involve increasing staff, adding new locations, and/or expanding a product portfolio with like products, etc.

In the early days of a business organic growth is what you have to pursue; you only need to think of the more sophisticated options (see pp. 131–4) once you have exhausted your existing capabilities, in terms of machinery, space, people, or whatever.

Organic growth is not without its challenges and pitfalls of course. Overextending yourself, or the business, is a common cause of difficulties. For example, creating a new factory or outlet requires investment. If you expand too rapidly you may find that the cost of the investment – in terms of any loans for instance – becomes too burdensome, and in the extreme you may see the downfall of your business. In an ideal world you will be able to grow using in-house funding, e.g. from profits from your existing business, and this makes the most sense. As soon as you have to go outside the business for funding then there is always a risk. That is not to suggest that numerous companies have not expanded exceedingly well using external finance, but once again it is a matter of being sensible and considering the downsides so that if things start going wrong, you are at least prepared.

TOP TIPS

■ Always do your homework prior to any investment for organic expansion

■ Determine whether the expansion can be phased pro rata to increased sales to minimize risks

9

Create your own opportunities

and recognize the threats

SWOTS IT ALL ABOUT

No matter what the development stage of the company it is never a bad idea to do a SWOT analysis. SWOT stands for Strengths, Weaknesses, Opportunities and Threats. It is a simple exercise but it focuses the mind. If you are developing a business plan you should always include a SWOT analysis, usually in the marketing section.

You need to be honest and insightful in the preparation of any SWOT analysis, since inappropriate or inaccurate information will inevitably generate false conclusions.

Likewise, in a growing company, the business plan is only a snapshot of the situation at a particular time, a bit like a balance sheet, so it never does any harm to review and update your SWOT at least annually.

For a successful company the entries in each category of the SWOT analysis might appear as shown in Table 9.1.

Table 9.1   What a SWOT analysis for a successful company might look like

Strengths

▶ Strong cashflow/cash reserves

▶ Excellent management team

▶ Fantastic product

▶ High margins

Weaknesses

▶ Difficult to identify any? In practice you need to be honest: there must be some and you need to identify them and fix them. Get someone close to you and acquainted with the business to be honest with you.

Opportunities

▶ Growing market

▶ Good, identified and qualified customers ready and keen to buy

Threats

▶ No competitors

▶ No major risks

For a floundering company, or one that is unlikely to ever get off the ground, the SWOT analysis might appear somewhat different as shown in Table 9.2.

Table 9.2   What a SWOT analysis for a floundering company might look like

Strengths

▶ Difficult to determine/none identified

Weaknesses

▶ Poor cashflow

▶ Poor/inadequate management

▶ Poor product

▶ Poor margins

▶ Declining or non-existent market

Opportunities

▶ Limited/none identifiable

Threats

▶ Lots of significant competitors

▶ Lots of risks, e.g. technical, financial, political, commercial, project, etc.

If you ever end up with an analysis that looks like the one in Table 9.2 you will need to rethink your strategy, since clearly your chances of succeeding are likely to be poor. You are unlikely to raise any money or, if using your own, there is a good chance you will lose it. Fortunately this book is all about addressing these real world problems, so maybe by the time you have finished reading and you redo the analysis, it might look more like the SWOT analysis for a successful company.

TOP **TIPS**

- Make sure your business has some major opportunities which can be realistically addressed, and some major strengths which will help you differentiate yourself from your competitors

- Work at reducing and eliminating any weaknesses, and always be mindful of competitive (and other) threats

10

Suppliers

RELATIONSHIPS

For many smaller companies developing a close relationship with suppliers is not exactly easy, for the simple reason that you are probably a small purchaser compared with your supplier's other customers. However, as you become a more significant customer to your supplier, the prospect of developing a closer relationship becomes possible and indeed essential.

Once you become a significant customer you need to develop a close mutual relationship whereby you both benefit from a win-win situation. For instance, if you commit to a certain minimum order level your supplier will probably be more prepared to offer you more competitive prices, and they may be prepared to offer bespoke products, better delivery times, better payment terms, etc.

TOP **TIPS**

■ A relationship with a supplier is a bit like marriage – it has its ups and downs – but good communications and common goals can help to mitigate the downsides

POOR QUALITY

Receiving poor quality products from a supplier is a real problem. First of all you need to ascertain whether the supplied goods meet any purchasing specification as laid down in the supply contract. If the purchased product meets the specification but does not meet your requirements then you have a problem. You have to see whether you can still use the product, or write it off, or perhaps talk the supplier into taking it back.

If the product does not meet the specification then you are on firmer ground: you should be able to demand supplies of the required quality meeting the agreed specification. It may be that the defect is only minor and that you could still, in practice, use the product, in which case it may be possible to negotiate a discount.

It may be, on the other hand, that you are receiving shoddy goods on a regular basis. In these circumstances you need to discuss with your supplier what is going wrong, encourage them to improve their quality control, etc. Offer a trial period during which they need to improve. If you are still unhappy then you need to consider going elsewhere.

If you do not have detailed purchasing requirements the chances are you are just relying on the supplier's published specifications, which may not be very comprehensive. In this situation you do not have a strong hand, but there is no harm in at least discussing the situation with the supplier, and seeing what you can negotiate.

It is always a good idea, whenever possible, to have a minimum of two suppliers, particularly if the quantities involved are large, so that you are never totally dependent on just one source.

TOP TIPS

- Ensure you specify the required quality when you order

- Don't accept goods whose quality is less than you are comfortable with – since it has a knock-on effect on your offering

- Use more than one supplier whenever economically sensible

DELIVERY DELAYS

Delays in the delivery of products from your suppliers can be quite problematic, especially if they impact on promises you have made to your customers.

When delays become systemic you need to talk to your supplier and determine their cause. Perhaps you need to assume an increase in the ordering time (i.e. assume a longer delivery time, maybe longer than the supplier is promising).

Financial penalties may apply against the supplier, but they seldom help you achieve your goal of keeping your customer satisfied.

If the problems persist consider changing suppliers – if this is possible.

TOP TIPS

- Always try to have more than one source of supply – that way if one supplier lets you down you still have at least one other option

- Communicate with your suppliers regularly – so that you can find out if they are going to be late in sufficient time for you to instigate a 'Plan B'

OUTSOURCING

Outsourcing has become very popular of late. It is when a business 'outsources' or subcontracts a task or function to another business which specializes in that task or function. For instance, we have all heard about call centres being outsourced, often to firms abroad who can offer the service at a much lower cost than can be achieved in the UK, and considerably less than if the task was carried out in-house.

Even though outsourcing is generally associated with larger businesses, it still has some merit even for smaller start-ups. There are a number of outsourcing options for start-ups which include:

▶ telephone reception

▶ payroll

▶ HR management

▶ transport

▶ secretarial services.

For outsourcing to be a success it helps to have considered the following:

1   Outsourcing strategy

    Never outsource key competencies

2   Relationship

    A close, trusting relationship with a long-term supplier is essential. You must trust your outsource partner and not be fearful that they will fail; you should not be looking over their shoulder all the time.

3   Rationale

    Cost is an important factor in deciding on outsourcing, but the strategic rationale needs to be the real reason, with financial savings following.

4   Back-off

    There is no point in outsourcing to a specialist only to tell them what to do all the time.

5   New ideas

    They should, as a specialist in their field, bring some of their own expertise to the relationship.

TOP **TIPS**

■ Make sure you do your homework thoroughly before committing to outsourcing, since once committed it is difficult to backtrack – especially if customer service has been adversely affected

■ Never outsource key competencies

■ Trust your outsourcing supplier

■ Allow the outsourcer to bring some expertise to the partnership

ENVIRONMENTAL ISSUES

If you feel particularly environmentally friendly for ethical and/or market-ing reasons, you need to determine what steps your supplier(s) are taking to avoid harming the environment. These include using minimizing energy consumption, using reusable materials, etc. You will, of course, be taking such steps yourself already – as an ethical and environmentally friendly business!

TOP **SUPPLIER TIPS**

■ Always look after your suppliers

■ Meet your suppliers frequently and tell them of your require-ments in good time. Do not impose sudden changes

■ Never take advantage of your suppliers!

11

Manufacturing and quality problems

Problems in manufacturing are legion and it is not surprising that the adage *'what can go wrong will go wrong'* is well known and understood among production people. The fact is that with the best will in the world and despite the best planning, design, etc., things still do go wrong, and often at the most difficult times.

For the production department this means products are either delayed or the quality is just not to the requisite standard. For the customer these issues can be significant. You can do what you can to improve the situation but if a customer was relying on your product being available at a certain time, and it isn't, then they are not going to be happy. The same situation will result if the quality is such that the product has to be returned or you provide the customer with an inferior service.

The bottom line is that these manufacturing problems can all too easily lead to customer problems, which can lead to cashflow problems – and worse! It is therefore unwise to:

▶ promise what you cannot deliver in a sensible timescale
▶ promise a quality level that cannot be met.

To minimize problems it is advisable, among other things, to:

▶ ensure delivery timescales are realistic, and if possible it is best to include some contingency (note: customers often feel good about you if their product arrives before the predetermined delivery date)

▶ ensure specifications are appropriate and can be attained.

Issues with the manufacturing problems of your suppliers are covered in Chapter 10.

TOP TIPS

■ Never promise what you can't deliver – either in respect of timescales or quality/performance

■ Always be aware of the saying 'what can go wrong will go wrong'

12

Information technology (IT)

Where would we be without computers these days? Most companies could not survive without them. IT also usually includes communications such as telephones, access to the internet, mobile phones, faxes, and so on.

The Business Link website provides an IT risk assessment tool which you might consider using. It should help you protect yourself against the most common IT-related risks (see Appendix 5 for website details – *businesslink.gov.uk/itrisks*).

So what are the issues around IT that could prove to be such a problem for your business? These might include any one or more of the following:

DATA SECURITY/THEFT

Companies have significant amounts of data on their computers, some of it very useful to competitors, and so data theft is a very real concern. Information can be stolen by an employee downloading data onto a disc, or physically printing it out onto paper, and passing it on to a third party. However, computer hackers can access your network and find the data readily via your internet connections or other telecoms links. Firewalls may help with low-level assaults but determined expert hackers can still often find a way in.

The only real solution where you have highly sensitive data is not to have the computers connected to any outside network, and to control staff access to those computers to minimize the prospects of theft.

Password security on each PC is also a must, although not a deterrent to the determined thief.

DATA SECURITY/BACK-UP

Computers are dependent on electricity but power failures can still occur, with a potentially adverse impact on the data stored on your computer. Likewise the advent of computer viruses, worms, etc., can mean that your computers can become infected, and in extreme cases, seize up, meaning your data becomes unusable.

The answer in all these cases is to back up your data. The safest way to do this is to have a physically separate hard disc drive and arrange for your computer data to be downloaded to the external drive at regular intervals and at least once per day for a business.

There are also specialist businesses which focus on providing remote back-up services using 'remote data vaults'. These types of service automatically back up your data at predefined intervals by encrypting and compressing it and sending it across the internet to a remote secure server, sometimes located in underground bomb-proof bunkers.

It has been estimated that small businesses can lose the equivalent of £20,000 per incident in lost business due to not backing-up regularly. Larger data-dependent businesses could be looking at over £10,000 per hour until service is restored.

DATA SECURITY/PERSONAL DATA

Under the Data Protection Act 1998 you must not hold personal data for any person without their permission. An individual has a right under the Act to check whatever information you hold about them.

In the case of staff most expect their company to keep their records on a computer, and this is often covered in the HR manual. Customers who are individuals are another matter however. Where you hold personal details of individuals on a computer you must ensure that you do not infringe the requirements of the Act. This will probably mean you need to register with the Information Commissioner's Office, and use the personal data only for defined lawful and approved purposes.

PHYSICAL SECURITY OF IT EQUIPMENT

Personal computers, laptops and mobile phones are all very saleable on the black market and hence are ready targets for thieves. All equipment should have security codes both well displayed and hidden, so that you can demonstrate to the police that any recovered property is in fact yours.

There are arrangements for fixing computers to desks. Laptops and mobiles are more difficult; staff should be encouraged to take responsibility for these items and they should be locked away in a drawer or office when not being used.

Remember that stolen computers and laptops can provide a thief with much useful data from the hard drive. You can ensure that you use the password protection and log-in facilities, which at least go some way to mitigating the situation, although these are no deterrent to the experienced thief/hacker.

COST OF IT EQUIPMENT

These days almost everyone in an office needs a PC. They need to be interconnected and there may well be a need for a separate server etc. If you include the telecommunications side of things with telephones, possibly with a small private branch exchange (PABX), then you can see how costs might escalate.

PCs can be purchased for anything from £500 to £1000 depending on the performance required. A telephone system can cost from £1,000 upwards. Good printers can cost from £200 upwards and so it goes on.

When preparing a business plan a figure of £1,000 per employee to cover IT set-up costs would not be inappropriate. To exclude such an allowance, or to get it significantly wrong, could make a difference between a profit and a loss in a year. You are advised to consult an IT expert if you have any doubts about what you might need and the associated costs.

On top of the initial purchase costs are the ongoing IT maintenance costs; we all seem to get glitches on our computers from time to time and all too often an IT expert is needed to fix the problem. You may well be fortunate to have a computer guru within your firm who can fix most problems, but if not, then you will have to pay to get you equipment working properly. There are firms who offer a maintenance service based on a monthly fee, which might be a good investment for many businesses, especially those particularly reliant on PCs and IT equipment generally.

MISUSE OF PCs BY STAFF

The misuse of PCs by staff is a topical issue. Misuse ranges from wasting time surfing the internet and sending e-mails to friends– to downloading pornography. Suffice to say the latter is unacceptable and illegal, and management needs to set very clear guidelines to staff as to what is and what is not acceptable (ideally in the HR manual).

If you are aware that pornography is being downloaded and effectively condone it by not doing anything about it, you could find your company ends up in hot water with a heavy fine, which is always a shock to the company finances. The moral is therefore not to allow inappropriate use of the company's IT facilities, to ensure that the company policy is clear to all staff, and to include the policy in the personnel handbook/manual.

MISUSE OF TELEPHONES AND MOBILES BY STAFF

Many staff see it is a perk, if not their right, to use company telephones and mobiles for personal calls. It is up to management to make clear what is acceptable, and what is not acceptable, company policy on this subject.

Remember that while telephone calls can be very cheap, some lengthy international calls and premium rate calls can cost £10, or more, per call.

These can easily build up and if left unaddressed could represent a significant monthly unbudgeted bill.

KEEPING UP TO DATE WITH SOFTWARE

Software is continually being updated and new releases are often launched every couple of years or so. With programs costing upwards of £200 a time the cost of using the latest software can be very expensive. Further, permitting an *ad hoc* approach, whereby different staff have different software releases, can invite problems with difficulties in downloading data between computers.

It is best to recognize that it is not usually feasible to keep abreast of every new software release (apart from free ones), and that judgements have to be made about the timeliness and cost-effectiveness of upgrading.

IT TRAINING

These days the young workforce generally comes IT literate. However there are still older people who may need training, or younger people who have slipped through the IT education net. Furthermore specific software packages, such as accounting or project management, may require specific training programmes since not all software can be learnt intuitively.

It is wise to budget a suitable amount for IT training as part of the overall company training budget if at all possible, and especially so for larger companies.

STAFF MOBILITY

More and more staff are mobile, or work from home. Many companies have salespeople on the road, for example mobile engineers, etc. In the 'old days' mobile staff sent their reports by fax back to the office, or even visited the office at intervals to make their reports.

Nowadays sophisticated mobile phones with e-mail capability, palm pilots and laptops can provide a mobile office on the move, with significant potential productivity savings combined with speed of communicating new orders, faults and so on.

Such equipment does not come cheap, however, especially if the company has a large number of mobile staff who can all justify having the equipment. Clearly if the productivity benefits justify the expenditure, then there should be no holding back, but you are advised to budget for such expenditure in advance if at all possible, so that there are no financial shocks to the system.

SPAM AND OTHER PROBLEMS

Spam is an unwanted e-mail message. Such messages can clog up a server and prevent wanted e-mails getting to you. Spam e-mails are also a common means of spreading viruses. They are best handled by a combination of firewalls, spam filters, and the latest anti-virus software.

Other problems are due to:

▶ Adware   programs which allow the delivery of (usually) unwanted advertising material to a computer and which are often downloaded without you realizing it

▶ Diallers   programs which are downloaded onto a computer connected to the internet via a modem, and which automatically call expensive telephone numbers, such as premium rate numbers, without the user knowing until they receive an abnormally high telephone bill

▶ Keystroke   programs which record the keystrokes logger made on a computer and send this information back to the hacker, who can then deduce passwords, etc., and can thus gain unauthorized access

▶ Malware   programs which are downloaded onto a computer without the user knowing, with the object of causing a computer malfunction

▶ Pharming   a variant of phishing, whereby bogus e-mails containing malware programs are installed on a computer so that when you type in a website address you are directed to a fake address. Sensitive information such as bank account information can thus be obtained

▶ Phishing   is the sending of bogus e-mails, which appear to be from trusted sources, but which are fraudulent and allow sensitive personal information to be obtained

▶ Spyware   programs, often hidden within freeware programs, which scan the contents of your computer without you knowing and access personal information

▶ Trojan horse   programs which appear to be legitimate but which allow unauthorized remote access to your computer

▶ Virus   programs which replicate themselves onto existing files and can cause anything from a mild malfunction to a complete system crash

▶ Worms   programs which infiltrate your computer and then replicate by sending copies of themselves to people listed in your e-mail address book.

TOP TIPS

- Make sure you comply with the Data Protection Act
- Take account of the reality of data and hardware theft before it happens
- Have a company policy against the use of offensive and inappropriate websites by staff
- Ensure you have an IT security policy including passwords, and change them regularly
- Ensure you have regular back-ups, ideally off-site
- Invest in high-quality firewall, anti-virus and e-mail filtering software

13

Intellectual property

Intellectual property (IP) is the process whereby an individual or company preserves their rights by filing or registering:

- ▶ a patent in the case of a particular invention or
- ▶ a copyright with respect to a document (i.e. a book, song, etc) or
- ▶ a trademark.

Patent filings are processed via the Patent Office. The precise cost varies according to whether you have your own patent lawyer, the countries to be covered, and so on. Searches have to be carried out to determine whether any similar patents have been filed. The Patent Office also checks that the innovation falls within the required parameters for a new patent, including being novel. The use of a registered patent agent is usually essential.

Protecting yourself with a patent means that no one else can use the idea without your agreement and without payment of a royalty unless, that is, you decide to provide a royalty-free licence.

Venture capitalists like to see lots of IP (i.e. patents) because they are perceived to have value, either in the present or downstream. Intuitively companies with lots of IP are seen to have great potential, with the prospect of being very successful.

If your company has not protected its IP and a competitor steals the idea, there is not usually any redress for the company. So registering your IP is definitely worth doing. However, it is still possible for a company to have problems – even when it has its intellectual property (IP) protected – for one or more of the following reasons:

1 The protected IP is stolen and litigation commences but is unsuccessful, resulting in heavy legal expenses which, in an extreme case, could drive the company to the wall.

2 The IP is protected but the company cannot afford litigation. The competitor takes the idea and the company collapses under the weight of the new competition.

It worth noting that it is perhaps easier for companies in the USA to enter into patent litigation because there are patent lawyers in that country who are more willing to work on a 'success fee only' basis, which avoids the problem of still having to pay a legal bill in the event that you do not win your case.

Many start-ups these days are created by universities, often with considerable IP, following much academic research. However data suggests that despite these start-ups being IP-rich, they have a below average success rate (around 15%). This indicates that having IP is not, of itself, a guarantee of success.

There are issues around what happens to the IP when a university spin-out fails. If there are no restrictions in any of the company's agreements an insolvency practitioner will sell the IP, along with the company's other assets, to the highest bidder, and they will be lost to the university. One option for the university is to allow the spin-out company to use the IP, but not actually assign the rights for a period of three years, by which time the company will either have been wound up or should be well on the road to success.

HOW TO PROTECT YOUR INTELLECTUAL PROPERTY

Copyright

In the case of drawings, artwork and literature you can apply a copyright to prevent others copying your IP. In principle you have the copyright of a document, etc., as soon as you write it, and you only need to mark each document with the copyright symbol, ©, and the year, although even this is not strictly required in the UK, but is required in certain other countries.

For complete peace of mind you should register the item as a trademark, and you need to speak to a trademark agent to perform this.

Patents

A patent needs to be taken out for an idea, concept, physical materialization of same, etc.

When granted a patent allows the holder to prevent others from using the protected invention. However, for a patent to be granted it has to be shown to be new and novel, and must involve some form of inventive step that was not obvious to a reasonably skilled person working in the field, and is not already known. The idea also has to be capable of being made to work.

You should contact a patent agent to register a patent (see the Chartered Institute of Patent Agents' website address in Appendix 5).

Trademarks

A trademark gives you exclusive rights to use the registered name in your particular business area. If you use a trademark which is already registered by another company you could face legal action from that company.

Some 80% of SMEs (small and medium size enterprises) have not registered the name of their business as a trademark!

If you have a simple trademark you may be able to register it yourself via the UK Government Patent Office (see website address in Appendix 5).

Alternatively you can use a trademark attorney (see Appendix 5 for the Institute of Trade Mark Attorneys' website)

CONFIDENTIALITY AGREEMENTS

When dealing with another entity, for instance another company, you should get them to sign a confidentiality agreement, or non-disclosure agreement (NDA), before disclosing any confidential or commercial information, ideas, or intellectual property.

Such agreements can be either two-way (or reciprocal), which means both parties agree to keep the information confidential, or one just way, where the information flow is just one way and only the receiving party agrees to keep the information confidential.

When using such agreements on a project where advisors will be used, for instance, lawyers, accountants, investment (mergers and acquisition) bankers, etc., it is always a good idea to ensure that any confidentiality agreement (or NDA) allows you to share the confidential information with these advisors, otherwise you could be in breach of the agreement.

Confidentiality agreements (and NDAs) give some degree of comfort, but it has to be said that if one party is a small business and the other a large corporation with deep pockets, if things were to go awry few small firms would be able to afford the legal costs of obtaining recompense.

TOP TIPS

■ If you've got something novel ensure you patent it

■ Copyright any documents of potential value

■ Don't be afraid to use confidentiality agreements

14

Health and safety

Health and safety is seen by some directors and businesspeople as an annoyance, something bureaucratic for which they have no time, and something to delegate to subordinates.

In the current environment this attitude is unacceptable, not least because directors are now held culpable for the safety of their staff, customers, and others who might be impacted by the activities of their company. If found guilty in a court of law the company can be fined £50,000 or even more, and the directors and senior managers can potentially be both fined and/or imprisoned, depending on the nature and seriousness of the incident. Such fines could lead to the downfall of a company, not just because of the magnitude of the fines but because of loss of credibility among customers, especially in the case of, for instance, a train operator.

Health and safety is therefore a topic of concern to all staff. The message about the importance of health and safety should come from the very top, which means the CEO has to be seen to be involved and taking the subject seriously.

One good way to ensure adequate visibility at the top is to have health and safety as an agenda item at board meetings. If you are a small business with no board, you should try to adopt health and safety principles as a way of life, and to reflect at intervals on what, if anything, you might do to improve things in this area.

For businesses with a top executive team, many experts are of the view that it is not a good idea to have a dedicated director, for the simple reason that everyone has responsibility for health and safety in their particular area of control. The thinking is that the only justification for having a designated member of staff is so that the company at least has an in-house expert who can advise other directors and staff members of their responsibilities and check that processes and procedures are in place and are being followed, etc. The parallel here might be with HR, where line managers have the responsibility for their staff but HR provides the specialist advice.

The Business Link website provides a tool which is aimed at helping businesses improve their health and safety performance (see website details in Appendix 5 – businesslink.gov.uk/healthsafetyindicator).

TOP **TIPS**

- Ensure the company has a well-publicized health and safety policy and appropriate procedures in place
- Demonstrate commitment at the very top by having health and safety as an agenda item at board meetings

15

Pensions

Pensions are a minefield and too detailed a topic to go into in any detail here. Suffice to say that companies have been known to collapse when pension planning goes awry. Companies with, for example, final salary pension schemes (where the company has to ensure the pension fund is adequately funded to meet the pension requirements) are particularly at risk, which is one of the reasons why such schemes are not often offered now to new employees.

For start-ups pension schemes are still an issue since staff expect them to be provided, and indeed the law requires that adequate arrangements are put in place. Pensions provision can be costly for a young, growing company, and the costs need to be factored into the business plan at the outset otherwise you could end up with some unforecast costs.

Pension-related problems for companies include:

▶ no, or inadequate, pension planning

▶ pension fund underfunding

▶ stock market underperformance leaving pension fund underfunded

▶ looting of pension fund by company (now illegal)

▶ adverse taxation.

You should seek independent professional advice on any matters pertaining to pensions. When choosing an independent financial advisor you would be well advised to seek recommendations, and speak to a number of advisors before making any final decisions.

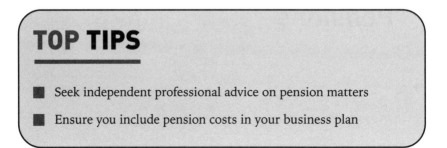

TOP **TIPS**

■ Seek independent professional advice on pension matters

■ Ensure you include pension costs in your business plan

16

Venture capital funding

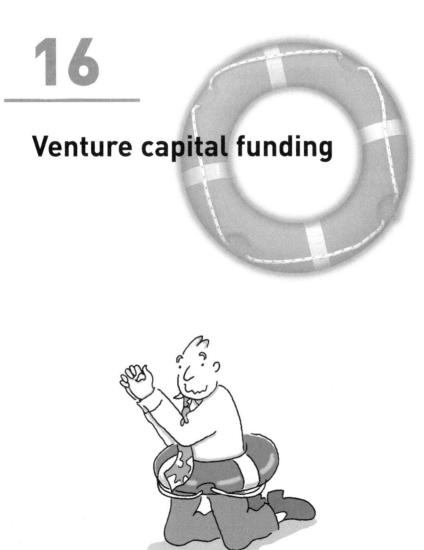

"Please may I have some money . . ."

WHEN TO USE VENTURE CAPITAL

Chapter 4 has outlined the various funding options. Venture capital is used by start-ups requiring typically £1M or more, although there are some who will invest less, as will venture capital trusts (VCTs). Venture capital firms will require a stake in the company in return for their investment.

WHERE TO FIND VENTURE CAPITAL

The British Venture Capital Association website (see Appendix 5) provides useful information on raising venture capital and, based on the information you provide, the site generates a list of VCs who might be interested in investing in your project, and who might therefore be worth contacting.

VC DESIRE FOR QUICK EXIT

The points in this section relate particularly to VC funding but may also, to a greater or lesser extent, apply to business angel funding.

VCs find their money from pension funds and other investment sources. The VC is then charged with making a return on that money as well as trying to make some money for themselves. For larger deals, where there is a history of revenue and profit growth, they may be able to leverage the transaction by also deploying debt capital, in the ratio of 2:1 (debt to equity) for example. For smaller deals and for start-ups this is unlikely to be the case.

VCs might raise a fund and plan to keep it open for, say, ten years. However, to ensure they meet the requirements of their investors, VCs tend to aim to achieve a satisfactory return on their investment in any company in which they might invest within, typically, three to five years. Accordingly, when reviewing your business plan, they will be looking at not only how much money they might make from the deal, but the timescale in which they might be able to make an exit. An exit means the VC is able to sell some, or all, of their stake in the company. Exits are usually achieved by a strategic/trade sale, a flotation (on AIM, Techmart, or the full stock exchange), or in a few cases by a secondary buy-out (where another VC buys the stake of the original VC).

STARTING UP – SOME CONSEQUENCES OF VC FUNDING

VCs require that you have skin in the game. This means that the VC will require you to invest in your own company to the extent that it will hurt personally if the company founders. The amount VCs like to see invested is not related to the amount that they put in, but more to what the founder(s) can reasonably just about afford; it may mean a founder having to remortgage the house, taking out a big bank loan, etc.

In the euphoria of finding funding it is worth just remembering that there is often major churn of the founders in the early years (see p. 77), and you need to factor in this possibility in the relevant company documentation in the drafting stages. For instance, as an investor you might wish to have stated in your employment contract (or other relevant documents) what happens to your stake (which you have personally paid for) and its valuation in the event of an earlier than anticipated departure from the company.

If you have taken out a bank loan to pay for your stake, you would be well advised to make sure that your salary, or other means, can adequately cover the monthly repayment costs, and give some thought as to what you would do if either you lost your position in the company or the company had to be wound up prematurely.

When seeking funding from VCs you will have to supply information to them, for instance about market size, potential customers, strategy, etc. The VC will require directors' warranties regarding the accuracy of this data. The penalty for supplying inaccurate data in this way can typically be up to three times your annual salary, so it is a sum which hurts if it has to be paid. It is therefore essential that you are scrupulously honest about your assessments, data, proposals and forecasts. Where possible you might consider substantiating your data by referring to reliable third party sources, e.g. independent consultants'/analysts' reports, etc. If there is any doubt about the accuracy of particular data then you should always make it clear that it may not be correct, or is subject to change, or cannot be substantiated, so that the VC knows not to put too much weight on it in its decision as to whether to fund or not (see also p. 121).

VCs ask you to declare any personal interests that you might have which might impact the business, and especially any conflicts of interest. Make sure that you do this because if they find out about any such situations downstream, may prove disastrous personally (see also p. 119).

VCs often carry out background checks on the founders. They will also take their own view about which of the founders is likely to make the best CEO, or whether they wish to introduce a CEO from outside, someone in whom they have confidence and who has the necessary experience and a successful track record. So it does not follow that just because you have had the bright idea for the business and have driven the project so far that you will become the full-time CEO once a VC is involved. This is often hard to swallow, but a fact of life if this sort of external funding is pursued. The same applies to some other key positions including chairman, finance director, and maybe the sales, technical and operations directors. The VC(s) will usually want to appoint one of more non-executive directors to the board – depending on their stake in the company. You could quite easily find that you have three non-executives on the board, possibly including the chairman, to complement the executive team of the CEO, the finance director, and maybe one other director.

It is advisable not to use the same lawyer as the VC. While this might in theory save some money, a single lawyer cannot genuinely look after the interests of both the VC and the founders. Select a lawyer who has been recommended and who has experience of start-ups and relevant business law.

Wherever possible make sure the legal fees are success based, and if acceptable to you and the lawyer is interested, you might reduce the cash cost of the legal fees by offering your lawyer warrants (or shares) in your company, representing say 50% of the fee, if the funding is successful.

Legal costs can be a particular problem for start-ups, since they can amount to anything up to perhaps £25,000, or even £50,000, depending on the work involved. These costs need to be factored into your calculations regarding the amount of money you need to raise from the VC.

For start-ups there are concerns that:

▶ if the VC decides not to invest after considerable legal work by your lawyers then, if you are unsuccessful in finding a replacement VC quickly and the legal fees are not on a success basis, you and any co-founders will be asked to pick up the tab while not having accomplished anything

▶ if you do find another VC to invest but there has been some excessive legal work then if the fees were not agreed on a fixed cost basis, they could escalate dramatically. This may not be too much of a problem if you raise the money you need and there is some slack in the budget, but otherwise it could be. You are advised to discuss this eventuality with your lawyer at the start of any work so as to minimize any surprises and to have a strategy for what you might do if your first VC does indeed back out – for whatever reason.

WHEN THINGS START TO GO WRONG

There are numerous things that can go wrong once the company has started following the raising of funding. VCs will make judgements all the time about the quality of the management team and their ability to ride the storms which will inevitably occur – that is what business life is about. However when things get really bad then more often than not the net effect is that the cashflow is adversely impacted, and then the VC is asked to stump up more money to keep the ship afloat. In these circumstances the VC's view tends to prevail and things sometimes get personal, especially as far as the CEO and some, or all, of the directors are concerned. At this juncture it is too late to realize that you do not have the best employment contract in the world! So it is prudent to be aware of a few things right at the beginning, even though in those early heady days the last thing you are thinking about is the company and/or your career going belly up.

When things start to go wrong there are a few things to be aware of, for example:

▶ The CEO often tends to take the can. The average life of a CEO of a start-up is reckoned to be around four years.

▶ For start-ups with less than two years in business the average life of a CEO is one to two years. Why is this? In some instances the founder – the one with the bright idea, might have been ideal for getting the show on the road, but may not have the experience or credentials to grow the business; therefore a change of CEO is sometimes considered necessary.

▶ In other cases the VCs, who generally have a major say at each round of funding, will have a view as to whether the incumbent CEO is the sort of person they want to have heading up their company. So it is not uncommon for CEOs to be replaced as part of a new funding round. Not necessarily because the incumbent cannot do the job, or isn't good, it may just be as simple as the fact that the VCs have a particular vision of the type of person they like to see as a CEO.

▶ For a CEO to leave in such circumstances is rather sad since it is they who, with co-founders, helped build the company to its present state. It is therefore highly desirable from the CEO's personal perspective to have an employment contract which allows for such eventualities and ensures that, assuming they are not incompetent/dishonest/fraudulent, etc., they do not leave entirely empty handed. In the old days a two-year notice period helped mitigate the situation for the departing CEO but in the light of recent corporate governance thinking, a 12-month notice period is now more likely, and is probably the most that is likely to be negotiated.

LOVE YOUR VC

Nobody likes surprises, and VCs are no different. They should be kept informed of progress, both good and bad, at least monthly. Major investors will probably have a seat on the board and should hear honest reports at monthly board meetings. Minor shareholders should also be appraised of progress, sometimes by regular briefings, e.g. quarterly, or by monthly reports and/or board meeting minutes if they ask for them, supplemented by *ad hoc* meetings in the event of a major incident.

Given the above you might be forgiven for thinking that the VC has a major say, once you have committed to go with them, even though they may not have a majority share. It is therefore very important to select a VC who has the same vision as yourself, with whom you get on well and feel happy that you can work with in all business matters, in bad times as well as good.

If you are fortunate enough to have more than one VC interested in your business you can hold a 'beauty parade' and select the one you think you can best get along with, and who will meet most of your conditions. It is a bit like a job interview, where you should be asking as many questions as the interviewer.

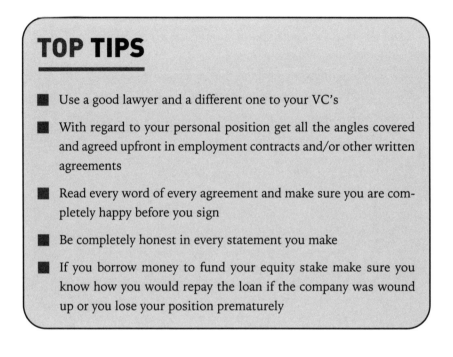

TOP TIPS

- Use a good lawyer and a different one to your VC's

- With regard to your personal position get all the angles covered and agreed upfront in employment contracts and/or other written agreements

- Read every word of every agreement and make sure you are completely happy before you sign

- Be completely honest in every statement you make

- If you borrow money to fund your equity stake make sure you know how you would repay the loan if the company was wound up or you lose your position prematurely

17

Corporate governance

There has been much publicity about corporate governance in recent years, especially following various major business disasters where large, well-known companies have gone to the wall. As a consequence much of the corporate governance reform of recent years has been focused on publicly quoted companies.

You may not see the need to worry about 'niceties' such as corporate governance when you are a start-up and in the formative stages of developing your business. Obviously a sole trader does not have to worry about their board of directors, public shareholders, and what the stock exchange might think or do about some action of theirs.

However if, as a start-up, you have aspirations to grow quickly, even as a private company, it does make sense to have appropriate corporate governance controls and procedures in place – as soon as is reasonably sensible and practicable in your particular business's circumstances. Indeed if you are looking to VCs for funding, they will be much more interested in your company if you can demonstrate that you have practical corporate governance procedures in place, or planned. Apart from anything else it shows that you know how a good company should be run, and suggests that you have aspirations to grow the business quickly.

Good corporate governance is all about the rights and responsibilities of a company's management, its Board of directors, its shareholders, and other stakeholders. Good corporate governance is important for companies looking for external funding because if companies are well run, they are more likely to perform well, and this in turn will enable them to attract investors who can help to finance faster growth. Poor corporate governance on the other hand may weaken a company's potential and, in the worst cases, can lead to financial difficulties, and even fraud.

The principles of good corporate governance also address issues such as conflict of interest, and the requirement for full disclosure, so as to ensure maximum transparency. Analysts, investment banks, auditors, accountants, lawyers, credit agencies, etc., should all avoid conflicts of interest which could compromise the nature of their advice. Indeed it is always prudent, as an example, to choose as your auditor a firm other than the one used to advise you on financial matters on a day-to-day basis.

A code of ethics should be published and there should also be an effective compliance programme to ensure that the code is followed. Furthermore individuals within companies who wish to highlight inappropriate behaviour or activities to the board, sometimes referred to as whistleblowers, should be able to do so in confidence.

The board of your company should always act objectively and independently, and be accountable to shareholders at all times. Boards should monitor and manage potential conflicts of interest, and be responsible for corporate ethics, compliance with laws of the land, and overseeing internal control systems such as accounting and financial reporting.

In the UK a 'Combined Code' for corporate governance has been published, which is overseen by the Financial Reporting Council. The main elements of the Combined Code are given below:

1   Every company should be headed by an effective board, which is collectively responsible for the success of the company.
2   There should be a chairman, whose responsibility is to run the board, and a separate chief executive, whose responsibility is to run the company. Furthermore no single individual should have unfettered decision making capability (for major business issues).

3 The board should have a balance between executive and non-executive independent directors such that no single individual can dominate its decision making.

4 There should be a formal and transparent procedure for the appointment of new board directors. This is usually achieved via the mechanism of a board subcommittee – known as the appointments committee.

5 There should be an audit committee, whose role is to monitor the integrity of the company's financial reporting, ensure the independence of the external auditor, and review the financial and other risks.

6 The remuneration of the directors is usually determined by the remuneration committee. The directors' remuneration should be sufficient to attract, retain, and motivate the directors to run the company successfully. A significant proportion of a director's remuneration should be linked to both the performance of the company and individual performance. The policy on executive remuneration should be clearly stated.

7 The board members should receive information about the performance of the company and any other matters in a timely manner and in such a form that they can discharge their duties appropriately.

8 The board should take time out annually to assess its own performance, as well as that of its committees and individual directors

9 All directors should be re-elected at regular intervals, subject of course to satisfactory performance to date.

10 The board should present a balanced and understandable assessment of the company's position and prospects in its annual (and where appropriate interim) reports.

11 The board should establish a system of internal controls to safeguard shareholders' investments and the company's assets.

12 There should be suitable communications channels established with shareholders, both private and institutional (where appropriate), so that information on company objectives and performance can be shared.

13 There should be an annual general meeting for quoted companies which all shareholders can attend.

TOP **TIPS**

- All companies, whether large or small, should aspire to the principles of good corporate governance

- For start-ups and smaller private companies – let common sense prevail in the event that not all corporate governance recommendations are appropriate for your business

18

Fraud

There are numerous types of fraud which can occur in a company. They all have the potential to make a big financial impact on your business and some of the more common are:

1   False accounting.

2   Asset misappropriation.

3   Trade fraud.

4   Investment fraud.

5   Insurance fraud.

6   Computer and e-fraud.

7   Card payment fraud.

Warning signs of what might provide scope for/indicate fraud in your business include:

▶ no management accounts and uncompleted chequebook stubs

▶ slow collection of debts

▶ reluctance to meet customers on the premises

▶ turnover varies, significantly out of phase with the market

▶ unduly high stock levels

- ▶ increasing debt turn
- ▶ lavish entertainment
- ▶ dominant MD/CEO with docile board
- ▶ high turnover of auditors and legal advisors
- ▶ excessive hours worked and poor delegation
- ▶ reluctance to take a holiday
- ▶ inadequate credit checks on customers
- ▶ inadequate checks on new staff
- ▶ poor checks on access to IT systems
- ▶ profits affected by unusual deals
- ▶ excessive payments for consultancy
- ▶ secrecy about a key client
- ▶ management unduly focused on share price
- ▶ aggressive accounting policies.

Ways to protect your business against fraud include the following:

1 Screen employees

   Make all necessary background checks and follow up references, especially for sensitive positions.

2 Train staff

   Ensure your staff are adequately trained in your standard procedures, and know what to do if there are any deviations.

3 Implement whistleblowing procedures

   Encourage, don't punish, whistleblowers, but be aware of the possibility of staff vendettas.

4 Use the courts when necessary

   If your company has been defrauded by an outsider try a civil action first. You can obtain a court order which enables assets to be traced and frozen.

5 Negotiate

As an alternative to the courts and especially if individuals are involved, you can try asking for any fraudulently obtained money to be repaid, stating that otherwise you will go to the police

6 Use technology

There are various technological options for minimizing fraud, for instance ability to recover deleted information from PCs, use of PIN numbers, etc.

7 Stay alert

Be aware of the possibility of fraud at all times and especially if things are not as normal as they should be, for instance suppliers' bills on the increase.

8 Two signatories for each cheque

Always have two signatories for signing cheques, and for authorizing payments via online bank accounts.

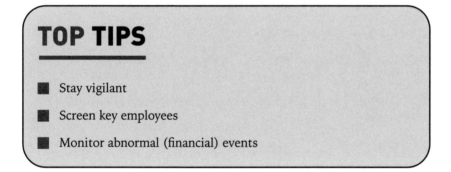

TOP TIPS

- Stay vigilant
- Screen key employees
- Monitor abnormal (financial) events

19

Disaster planning

This chapter is not intended to be unduly pessimistic or to put you off start-ing your own business, but there is so much that can go wrong that it is amazing that any company actually survives.

Of course, it is because things do not normally pan out as planned that start-ups tend to suffer from 'disasters' more than older companies. This is not necessarily due to the fact that the start-up entrepreneur lacks drive or experience, but more that the business lacks the momentum, financial reserves and other resources of a larger company which can often ride the waves more successfully than a smaller one when things go wrong (although even this is not always the case).

It does help however to have contingency plans in place so as to mitigate the effects of as many disasters which might occur as possible. Such disas-ters might include:

▶ a long spell of inclement weather, e.g. floods, storms, snow, earth-quake, hurricane, etc., which might affect your ability to produce/sell and generate revenues

▶ no electricity, or other utility service, for a long period

▶ staff sickness, e.g. widespread epidemic of flu

▶ war (heaven forbid)

▶ fuel restrictions, e.g. petrol limited in supply and/or price going through the roof

▶ terrorist alert or disaster

▶ fire, explosion

▶ serious multiple staff accident

▶ collapse of IT systems.

The bottom line is that it is always a good idea to have a contingency plan and all companies, including start-ups, should have such a plan written down and updated annually, and have a disaster management team which can be activated at such times. (NB: it is recognized that start-ups have more than enough to do in the early stages without worrying about contingency plans, but they are nevertheless well worth considering as soon as is practicable.)

There is a good reason as to why contingency plans are a good idea: Gartner Research has suggested that as many as 40% of companies suffering a disaster go out of business within five years – so it pays to ensure you are one of the 60% who do not – by being prepared with realistic contingency plans for each of the disasters identified above. The obvious objective is to mitigate the downside of any major negative event.

TOP TIPS

■ Take time to plan ahead for the more common disasters

20

Realizing your assets

If you have a good product/service, have operated in a buoyant market, have not had too many problems along the way, together with a good slice of luck, after a few years you may have grown your business into quite an attractive profitable operation. Indeed it might be so attractive that it might be very saleable. Alternatively you may be thinking about retiring and selling up.

There are three main methods of realizing the value locked up in your company, namely:

▶ trade sale
▶ sale to a venture capital house
▶ flotation on AIM, or even the full stock market.

Entrepreneurs and business owners vary somewhat in terms of their desires and aspirations for the future. Some have started their business and want to run with it until they retire. Others have it in mind to pass the business on within the family, but still retain a back seat.

There are some who, while totally devoted to growing their business over a period of some years, are not so wedded to it that they would not sell it if a sufficiently high price was offered for it. They say everyone has their price, and in business this is most certainly the case.

All sorts of businesses can be sold. However the real question is, 'How much can it be sold for'? Some businesses are definitely more exciting than others, and if you are in a so-called 'hot' sector then your operation might well sell at a healthy premium, possibly even irrespective of its revenues and profitability. It might be attractive to a potential buyer for many reasons including, perhaps, your company having a synergistic product, or premises that fit in well with the purchaser's other locations.

Businesses which are not growing significantly year on year, or which maybe are not growing at all, are unlikely to achieve particularly attractive selling prices.

The value of a company can be determined in many different ways, but the sale price that you might actually achieve is very much a factor of the perceived value on the part of the buyer. The buyer might see a retail business which is plodding along, but has ideas about how to grow it rapidly, knows the market is there, and has the cash to inject to make it really successful. The buyer doubtless would not offer much of a price based on the revenues and profits of this retail outlet, but might be sufficiently keen to pay an attractive premium if it has something that they perceive as being valuable, e.g. product, location, customer base, etc.

Sometimes businesses are approached out of the blue by a potential buyer, or via their advisors, and often a good fair deal can be negotiated following such an approach.

More typically, however, the owner(s) decide to test the market and approach advisors. There are broadly two categories of advisor:

1   There are firms that specialize in selling smaller companies, typically shops and other small businesses with annual revenues up to around £1–2M p.a. Some such firms advertise in business magazines, financial newspapers, in the business sections of the Sunday newspapers and on the internet.

2   For larger companies most investment banks have mergers and acquisitions departments which specialize in such deals. There are also various boutique finance houses which can handle corporate sales. Smaller and/or growing firms can still be of interest to the large investment banks if the sale price is sufficiently large. For instance a high-tech firm

may have relatively low revenues and profits, but may be worth £50M or more, due to perhaps to having a valuable portfolio of patents, or having valuable customer contracts, etc., which together might suggest a valuable high-growth company. The fees for selling a company can be anything up to 7% of the selling price, but the experience and negotiating skills of experts may well mean that a higher selling price could be achieved than might otherwise be the case.

If the ultimate goal is to sell the company within a certain timeframe, and if you have venture capital backers this will be a definite requirement, then you do need to plan well ahead if you are to maximize the selling price. VCs typically look for an exit whereby they can recover their investment and obtain a capital gain (typically three to five times their original investment) within a three to five year timeframe.

Companies for sale are valued in many different ways, depending on the nature of the business, for example:

▶ net asset value

▶ multiple of the annual revenues, or even forecast revenues

▶ price to earnings ratio (multiple of profits – the precise multiple varying depending on the sector)

▶ future profits (using discounted cashflow to bring value back to present day)

▶ 'enterprise value'

▶ what someone will actually pay (which may bear no resemblance to any of the above).

The first four can all be determined from the company accounts. Enterprise value is used more for traded companies since it is calculated by taking the market capitalization (i.e. share price × number of shares issued) plus all debt, less cash, and less any investments. It is a measure of the real value of a company as an enterprise rather than just one of pure market capitalization.

If you are thinking of selling your company, or have been approached regarding a sale, it is important that you retain appropriate advisors who will ensure you get the best possible price and also help you avoid any pitfalls.

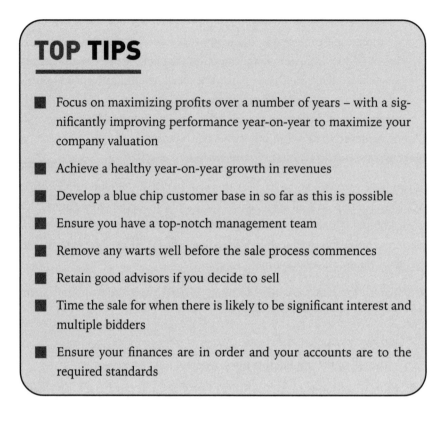

TOP **TIPS**

- Focus on maximizing profits over a number of years – with a significantly improving performance year-on-year to maximize your company valuation

- Achieve a healthy year-on-year growth in revenues

- Develop a blue chip customer base in so far as this is possible

- Ensure you have a top-notch management team

- Remove any warts well before the sale process commences

- Retain good advisors if you decide to sell

- Time the sale for when there is likely to be significant interest and multiple bidders

- Ensure your finances are in order and your accounts are to the required standards

PART THREE

When things do not go according to plan

21

If it all goes horribly wrong

Regrettably, as stated right at the beginning, around a third of businesses do not survive beyond their third year. This book has highlighted the numerous pitfalls which can beset any business and has provided ideas for avoiding and mitigating them. It would be gratifying to think that if you have read this book you will not find yourself in such difficulty that you decide you need to wind up your business prematurely.

However, there may be some for whom advice is already too late, so what are the options?

Well, first of all, don't bury your head in the sand, since the problem will not go away. Seek advice from your accountant and maybe your lawyer to determine whether they can offer any help, even at this stage.

Depending on the nature of the problem and how far down the road you are, you may or may not be able to salvage something. As mentioned many times in this handbook the usual reason for thinking of having to wind up a business is that you either are running out, or have run out, of cash. Clearly in such circumstances the quick fix is to find some cash from somewhere. All the usual sources as mentioned in Chapters 2, 4, and 16 might be considered as appropriate. If the shortage of cash is due to some form of hiccup, or temporary problem, then all may not be lost and your bank may be able to help, which is why it is always a good idea to maintain good relations with your bank manager/relationship manager. If the company still has great future prospects, then VC funding may still be a possibility. However, if there are irresolvable problems then finding additional funding may be difficult.

Also, even if you were able to find additional funding, you must ask yourself whether you are only putting off the evil day, and whether it might not be best to wind up now rather than prolonging the agony! To carry on you must genuinely be satisfied that the new financing will enable you to turn the business around.

For sole traders, proprietors and partners, you might consider contacting your local branch of the Citizens' Advice Bureau (see contact details in Appendix 5), who are able to advise individuals with financial difficulties. They will refer you to one of their financial experts and it may just be that they will be able to see a way ahead for you which does not mean the demise of your business. If it appears that there is no viable alternative then they may put you in touch with an insolvency practitioner.

The remainder of this chapter applies to companies, rather than sole traders or partnerships. When things get tough as a company, there are serious legal issues which you need to be aware of. Put simply, as a director of a company, it is illegal to allow the company to trade insolvently, which means you cannot commit to expenditure if there is no reasonable expectation that you can pay the bill. There are severe penalties for directors who do not play by the rules, with fines, disqualification from holding a company director's position in the future, and even imprisonment for the worst cases.

If you find yourself in a position of being about to trade insolvently, then seek professional advice urgently. In the event that you are advised to liquidate the company there are a number of different insolvency procedures, and their outcomes for shareholders and staff can be very different, depending on which route is chosen. The various routes are explained below. Appendix 2 also provides practical data about the outcomes of different insolvency approaches and it would be advantageous to understand the implications of these different options at the earliest opportunity although, even armed with this information, you must take the advice of a qualified insolvency practioner.

Apart from a straightforward winding-up – which applies when there are no creditors – the different insolvency categories are:

▶ compulsory liquidation

▶ administration

▶ corporate voluntary arrangement (which can be either a members' voluntary liquidation or a creditors' voluntary liquidation). This is where a company makes an agreement with its creditors, which is agreed by a court, for the settlement of its debts.

▶ receivership.

For any of these you need professional advice, usually from an insolvency practitioner, and your accountant can usually put you in touch with one. The Companies House website also provides invaluable guidance, as does R3, the Association of Insolvency Practitioners (see Appendix 5 for details).

WINDING-UP – WITH NO DEBTS

'Striking off' (the Companies House register) is the term used when the company is no longer trading and there is shareholder agreement that it should be wound-up, and there are no outstanding debts. This situation is not insolvency but is included for completeness, since there will be some companies who just want to call it a day and wind up the business, but are still able to pay all outstanding debts.

In an ideal world, if you can see that things are coming to an end, the best outcome is that you wind-up the company with the agreement of the shareholders and leave no debts. This is by far the cleanest outcome and avoids the cost of expensive lawyers, etc. You can then apply to Companies House to have the company struck off, for which only a nominal fee is required.

COMPULSORY LIQUIDATION

Compulsory liquidation typically occurs when a court orders that the company be wound-up, following a petition of one or more creditors on the grounds that it cannot pay its debts. The official receiver is formally appointed and has the duty to investigate the company's affairs and the causes of its failure. However, the official receiver typically arranges the appointment of a liquidator, who then has the practical task of winding-up the company.

If the assets of the company are such that they are unlikely to cover the costs of winding-up, and no further investigation of its affairs is necessary, the official receiver may apply for early dissolution of the company.

ADMINISTRATION

If you have to wind-up the company and there are outstanding debts, but selling the business might raise sufficient funds to pay them, then administration may be the best way ahead. This is because it provides a chance for the company to survive, albeit in a modified form, and for creditors to maximize the chance of debts being repaid. In this situation an administrator (an insolvency practitioner) is either appointed by the court to run the company for the benefit of the creditors, or the directors can appoint one directly if they so wish, although if a bank holds a floating charge it will often be able to appoint its own administrator. Soon after the appointment of the administrator, they decide whether some or all of the management team should depart, and it is not uncommon for many of the top team and the CEO/MD to be out of a job almost immediately.

The role of the administrator is to achieve the most favourable outcome for the creditors, hence they usually look to see whether they can achieve a better price for the company's assets than would otherwise be the case. This can be achieved by, for instance, selling it as a whole to another company, or maybe to VCs, for a sufficient amount to repay the debts, and any remaining money returned to shareholders on a pro rata basis. If the administrator cannot sell the company as a whole, they will see whether they can sell parts of it: failing this they will dispose of the assets, e.g. plant and machinery, buildings if owned, etc.

Of particular note is that any pending winding-up petitions will be dismissed or suspended and there will be a moratorium on any insolvency or other legal proceedings pending the outcome of the administration process.

After eight weeks of the administration process the administrator must make a statement setting out proposals for achieving the purpose of the administration or explaining why they cannot be achieved. Any such proposals may include a voluntary arrangement, or an arrangement with creditors or members, or some other acceptable compromise.

Administrators can be quite successful, in which case the company may be able to continue trading either as a whole, or as a reduced entity. In the worst case the company is forced into liquidation, in which case the shareholders generally see little of their money.

The administration process may end when it is decided that the company should either proceed with a creditors' voluntary winding-up, whereby creditors obtain some or all of their money back, or be dissolved, which occurs when there are no funds available to be repaid to creditors.

The formal legal processes for administration and subsequent liquidation can take many years (as many as four to five) before everything is sorted out and the company laid to rest.

Company directors need to be aware that the administrator has to submit a report to the Department of Trade and Industry regarding the performance of the directors in the three-year period leading up to administration. In particular they look for evidence of trading while insolvent, failure to keep proper accounting records, failure to prepare and file accounts and make returns to Companies House, and failure to submit tax returns and pay any tax due. Directors can find themselves before a court for serious breach of regulations and laws.

Where administration appears to be unlikely to help the situation then immediate liquidation can occur.

VOLUNTARY LIQUIDATION

There are two types of voluntary liquidation:

1   Members' voluntary liquidation

In this case the directors make a statutory declaration of solvency that they have made a full inquiry into the company's affairs and that it is their belief that the company will be able to pay all its debts within 12 months from the start of the winding-up process. The members (directors) need to pass an appropriate resolution at a general meeting stating that the company cannot continue in business because of its liabilities and inability to pay its debts. The resolution is then advertised in *The Gazette* (used by lawyers, insolvency practitioners, etc. for making legal announcements) and a liquidator is appointed to wind-up the company's affairs. They do this by calling in all the company's assets and distributing them to its creditors, and anything that might be left over is returned to the members of the company.

2   Creditors' voluntary liquidation

In this case the directors will not have made a statutory declaration of solvency but instead an agreement with the creditors, which has to be approved by the Court, for repaying all or part of the debt. A corporate voluntary arrangement can be made by an administrator – if there is an administration order in place, or by a liquidator – if the company is to be wound-up, or by the directors in certain other circumstances.

RECEIVERSHIP

There are many types of receivership. An administrative receiver is appointed by, or on behalf of, the holders of any debentures of the company secured by a floating charge, and has the power to sell or realize, the assets covered by the floating charge, and applies the proceeds to the debt owed to the charge-holder.

Other types of receiver may be appointed, for instance under the powers contained in an instrument or document creating a charge over a company's property until the debt is recovered, e.g. a bank loan where there is a charge on certain assets.

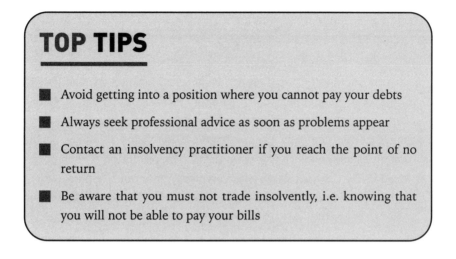

TOP **TIPS**

- Avoid getting into a position where you cannot pay your debts
- Always seek professional advice as soon as problems appear
- Contact an insolvency practitioner if you reach the point of no return
- Be aware that you must not trade insolvently, i.e. knowing that you will not be able to pay your bills

PART FOUR

It's a wrap

22

Help is at hand

Everything about business moves fast and nothing stays the same for long. There is a need for an ever-increasing awareness of legislation in areas such as employment, taxation, and health and safety, to name a few.

Fortunately there are lots of ways of keeping up to date which are not too onerous. You might wish to consider the following:

CONFERENCES AND SEMINARS

The Institute of Directors, for instance, arranges numerous conferences, courses, seminars and local events throughout the year, targeted at company directors to help them keep up to date in all requisite areas (see contact details in Appendix 5).

Other organizations which run courses include Business Link and local Chambers of Commerce, so it pays to keep in touch with these bodies too.

TRADE ASSOCIATIONS AND PROFESSIONAL INSTITUTIONS

Trade bodies, professional institutions and local Chambers of Commerce often have networking events which are excellent ways of meeting other like-minded businesspeople and enable you to keep up to date on developments in your industry or market, and on the latest legislation and professional development.

Some of the organizations which might be of interest are listed in Appendix 5.

PROFESSIONAL ADVISORS

You should not forget professional advisors such as lawyers and account-ants. While of course you can always pay for their services, many such advi-sors, as part of their marketing campaigns, send out newsletters and updates which provide the latest information on topics such as employment law, latest tax developments, etc. Some advisors even have free seminars. It is worth keeping your eyes open for such things in your local area.

MAGAZINES (HARD AND ELECTRONIC FORMATS)

There are a number of excellent business magazines which include:

Director Magazine	published by the Institute of Directors
Business XL	published by Vitesse Media (you can register online at www.businessxl.co.uk)

WEBSITES

There are a number of very good business-focused web-sites which provide thought-provoking ideas and up-to-date information. These include:

www.is4profit.com

www.businessgo.co.uk

www.smallbusiness.co.uk

www.newbusiness.co.uk

www.bbc.co.uk

In addition the Business Link website also provides the latest business information (see Appendix 5).

TELEVISION AND RADIO

Business is becoming a popular subject among broadcasters and there are now a number of very popular programmes about funding of start-ups including the BBC's 'Dragons' Den' and Channel 4's 'Making It' series. BBC 2 also has a regular 'Working Lunch' programme of interest to business-people.

MENTORS

Research has indicated that start-ups which have a business mentor are more likely to survive for the long term than those that do not. Obviously the need for a mentor varies according to the expertise and track record of the entrepreneur but if you have not operated at board level in a company prior to starting up your business, then the chances are you could benefit from such a person. Even if you have worked at a senior level previously it sometimes helps just to have an independent third party to share your thoughts and problems with from time to time.

Larger companies often obtain this mentoring help by, in effect, appointing non-executive directors, but this may not be appropriate for most small firms and sole traders.

Some mentors, for smaller businesses especially, are freely available. This may sound unlikely in this day and age, where it seems you have to pay for everything. For people up to the age of 30 looking to start up their own business and seeking modest funding of up to £5,000, The Prince's Trust can be of help (see website details in Apendix 5). As a condition of providing any loan it is a requirement that the young entrepreneur take on a business mentor, whose services come absolutely free. The mentor usually meets them monthly, monitors progress, and helps advise on any problems, etc.

For other start-ups and for more established businesses, Business Link and other similar organizations can offer mentors. Here the mentors will discuss your objectives and goals and work with you to develop a plan to make it all happen, offering advice as necessary, with meetings as frequently or as seldom as you like (see Business Link website details in Appendix 5 or the equivalent body for your region). The Business Volunteer Mentor programme provides business mentors who give their services free; this service is operated by local Enterprise Agencies and other business support organisations.

23

Emotional roller-coaster

Starting and running a business is a non-stop emotional roller-coaster. It helps to recognize and be prepared for this phenomenon.

You start with the excitement of having a new idea, which you are convinced is going to be really successful. You then prepare your business plan and, more often than not, find that there are some not insignificant hurdles to overcome. Having addressed these you have all the practicalities of getting the show on the road, one of the major ones often being raising funding. It is not uncommon for entrepreneurs to have their business plans rejected numerous times by potential funders, resulting in emotional lows. However, by modifying the plan, the funding amounts needed, and maybe who you seek funding from, hopefully you eventually find a suitable funder. Back to a new emotional high.

Then you go through the legal phase which can quite often throw up some further difficulties, such as your funder wanting more equity or imposing unacceptable conditions and, despite the earlier high, you are back to a new low!

With some tenacity and good negotiating, together with taking some advice from professionals, you are able to overcome these hurdles.

You get your money and the business activity starts in earnest – a real high!

But then perhaps, after a few weeks or months, you realize that the customers are not generating the sales that you had predicted, and you forecast a disaster if you are not able to turn things around quickly – a new low.

Maybe you start recruiting some staff and everything looks really good, but then you start to have employee problems, e.g. if they are not pulling their weight. Can you sack them, should you try to develop them, do you have time for all this? Another emotional low develops.

Of course, having read this book you know all about the problems that can beset start-ups, so you have many of the answers; maybe you have also picked up a mentor along the way who also provides valuable advice. You are back to a new high!

And so it goes on. Even once you have been trading for some time there are numerous pitfalls which can still bring about new despondency. On the other hand there are also those successes, like winning major new business, which create real elation.

What you have to appreciate is that this emotional roller-coaster is quite normal, and you are very lucky if you do not experience it.

The trick is to:

▶ understand that you will almost certainly be on the roller-coaster

▶ recognize it for what it is

▶ be tenacious

▶ seek professional advice whenever appropriate, and

▶ work out the solutions to get you out of trouble.

It is really all about *'managing expectations'*.

24

Some final words of advice

1   Being an entrepreneur and starting a company requires tenacity, passion and commitment. However, do not pursue your entrepreneurial dream to the complete exclusion of your loved ones. Should you be less than successful they will still be there for you to help you pick up the pieces. Of course they will also be there to share in your success.

While toiling long hours, reflect occasionally on whether both you and your loved ones would not be better off if you had a little bit of a break now and again, and spent some time together – if only to recharge your batteries.

A final observation is that many a marriage/partnership has not survived a start-up situation because the entrepreneur has forgotten about their other love in life. You have been warned!

2   It takes time, sometimes as much as one to two years, to make a start-up fully operational (what with all the business planning, market research, fund raising, etc., that needs to be done), before you are in a position to even think about taking orders and receiving revenues. You are therefore well advised to carry out the preliminary start-up planning activity (i.e. writing business plans, raising funding and so on) from a position of financial security, by which I mean do not give up the day job prematurely.

3   Surviving the first three years is crucial for long-term success.

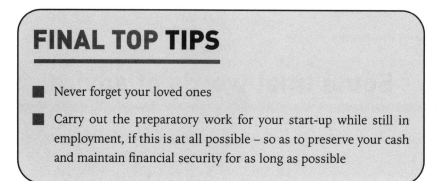

FINAL TOP **TIPS**

■ Never forget your loved ones

■ Carry out the preparatory work for your start-up while still in employment, if this is at all possible – so as to preserve your cash and maintain financial security for as long as possible

❝Reaping the rewards of success❞

25

Feedback

I hope this book has been a source of practical advice and inspiration. Doubtless there will be improvements which can be made and, like all good managers, I would be pleased to hear from readers with constructive suggestions as to any amendments, corrections, or items which could be added for future editions.

Email me at: *startup@pearson.com*

Appendix 1
Background business data

First of all a health warning regarding business start-up statistics! Businesses come in many different forms including companies, partnerships and sole traders. The nature of these enterprises is such that they do not all need to register their activities in the same way and so, perhaps surprisingly, there is no central UK database covering all businesses. Registrations for companies are via Companies House, businesses registered for VAT are registered with Revenue and Customs, and banks have data on those businesses, sole traders, partnerships and companies that have business accounts with them. However, many of the self-employed fall outside these formal methods of registration/calculation, since many use private rather than business bank accounts. So really precise comprehensive data about business numbers, especially smaller businesses, is not easy to establish. Furthermore the data does vary from year to year and from region to region. I have chosen to use ballpark figures since, for the purposes of this book, we only need generalized data to indicate the orders of magnitude; those requiring precise data for particular years can obtain it from the sources given in Appendix 5.

The DTI Small Business Service (SBS) provides data based on VAT registrations; Companies House provides data on company registrations; and Barclays Bank provides data based on business bank accounts.

In 2004 there were deemed to be approximately 4.3 million businesses in the UK, the highest ever figure, but rather amazingly only 6,000 companies employ more than 250 people. Put another way, over 99% of British businesses employ less than 250 people, so maybe the description of the British being a nation of shopkeepers, where 'shopkeepers' alludes to small business, is indeed true. Many of the 6,000 larger organizations are public limited companies, and many are quoted companies on the UK stock exchange, although there are some well-known ones, which are neither plcs nor quoted. Where these larger companies trade or have operations overseas, they are referred to as multinational corporations (MNCs).

The remaining businesses, that is almost 4.3 million, are what are called small and medium size enterprises, or SMEs, and the number of such companies has grown by some 15% over the last eight years.

Of the 29 million employed people in the UK, 23 million are employed in the private sector. SMEs employ just over half of this number with some 12 million staff. The public sector has some 6 million employees.

Companies House has a total of approximately 1.9 million companies on its register, with around 330,000 new companies added and 190,000 removed in a typical year.

There are approximately 1.8 million businesses registered for VAT in the UK, suggesting that the remainder, i.e. some 2.5 million, either have revenues below the current VAT threshold of £60,000 p.a., or perhaps are not trading.

Table A1.1 Summary of all UK businesses by size

Businesses/ Enterprises	Employees per business	Employees per category	Number of businesses
Small	0		3,100,000 (72.1%)
	1–50	10.3M	1,169,000 (27.2%)
Medium	51–250	2.6M	26,000 (0.6%)
Large	>250	9.1M	6,000 (0.1%)
Total		22.0M	4.3M

Businesses with no employees are sole traders/proprietors and partnerships, all of which comprise only the self-employed owner-manager, and companies with one (or more) non-employed director(s).

Table A1.2 Summary of UK registered businesses

Registered companies (i.e. ltd, plc, and llp)	Companies House (no. of businesses)	VAT registered (no. of businesses)
Small	1,868,000 (99.3%)	
Medium	26,000 (0.6%)	
Large	6,000 (0.1%)	
Total registered companies	1.9M	1.8M

The difference in totals for Companies House and the VAT register is simply that not all companies need to register for VAT, either because they are not trading or because their revenues are below the VAT threshold. On the other hand it is also worth noting that many businesses voluntarily register for VAT even though their turnover is less than the VAT threshold, and typically around 25% of all VAT registered companies are in this category.

Table A1.3 Summary by type of business in UK

Type of business	Percentage with employees	Number of businesses
Sole proprietor/trader	12.1%	2.72M
Partnerships	37.3%	540,000
Companies	61.8%	1.02M
Total		4.3M

The number of new businesses started up in any given year varies, and depends to some extent on the economic climate of the country as a whole. Typically in any single year it is thought that there are some 450,000 new businesses created, around 75% of which are companies registered at Companies House.

The number of businesses wound-up in a year is around 320,000, so generally speaking there is a slow net increase in the total number of businesses year on year. Many of the companies which are wound-up are ceased for non-financial reasons, e.g. the owner retiring, others will be for reasons such as the owner not being able to commit sufficient time to the venture, owner becoming employed by another business, or simply because the business is not making sufficient headway and the owner decides to call it a day.

Companies House removes around 190,000 companies from its register each year, but not all these are due to liquidation. Typically around 0.7% of active companies go into liquidation each year. It is thought that some 85% of company liquidations are for financial reasons, and invariably because there was insufficient cash available to continue.

On a positive note, and rather interestingly, since the 1950s about 50% of all innovations and 95% of radical inventions have come from SMEs. These enterprises are clearly a very important part of the business sector that the government and others neglect at their peril.

Appendix 2
Corporate insolvency

(Data and charts for this chapter have been taken or derived from the UK Government Insolvency Service website, and R3, the Association of Business Recovery Professionals 12th Corporate Insolvency Survey, which is available at www.r3.org.uk with their permission.)

GENERAL

This appendix is included so that you will have a basic knowledge of the causes of, and reasons for, insolvency, for two important reasons:

1   Armed with the information about how others have been less than successful, you will be able to avoid such an outcome for your business.

2   In the event that you are a creditor of another business which has gone into liquidation, you may want to lobby for an insolvency procedure which might maximize the chances of you getting at least some of your money back.

TOTAL INSOLVENCIES EACH YEAR

In a typical year there are around 12,000 company liquidations and over 36,000 individual business-related bankruptcies, and the numbers for both are increasing steadily.

The numbers of each different type of company insolvency procedure are given in Table A2.1.

Table A2.1 Analysis of UK company liquidations in 2004

Insolvency type	Insolvency sub-category	Number	Percentage of total
Liquidation	Compulsory liquidation	4,584	27%
	Creditors voluntary liquidation	7,608	44%
Insolvency proceedings	Receivership	864	5%
	Administrator appointed	1	0%
	Voluntary arrangements	597	4%
	In administration	457	2%
Other proceedings	Members voluntary liquidation	3,172	18%
Total		17,283	100%

Source: Derived from data on the UK Government Insolvency Service website

It should be noted that the split of insolvency types has changed with time and, in particular, the number of receiverships has reduced to almost zero in recent years due to changes in legislation and the relative popularity of the 'in administration' option.

REASONS FOR INSOLVENCY

Loss of market is the biggest cause of insolvencies, and typically accounts for 33% of all cases. Perhaps surprisingly and contrary to general public perception, insolvencies due to losing the bank's support represent a mere 6% – so banks are by no means always to blame for pulling the plug.

The remaining 60% or so of insolvencies are management related. Management inadequacies account for some 33% of the total, management inability to ensure adequate margins represents another 17%.

With such a high proportion of insolvencies being down to poor management, where shareholders are separate from management, shareholders need to be aware of the need to take any necessary action to improve performance earlier, rather than later, if they are not to lose out.

Table A2.2 lists the different types of business failure.

Table A2.2   Analysis of causes of insolvency

Failure	Percentage of total failures
Loss of market	34%
Bad debts	5%
Loss of long-term finance	5%
Loss of working capital or cashflow	13%
Fraud	3%
Over-optimistic planning	3%
Imprudent accounting	3%
Lack of management information	4%
Erosion of gross margin	13%
Excessive overheads	5%
New venture/expansion/acquisition	5%
Product obsolescence/failure	0%
Domino effect following another insolvency	7%
Total	100%

Source: Derived from data on the UK Government Insolvency Service website

DOES LOCATION OF COMPANY AFFECT LIKELIHOOD OF INSOLVENCY?

The statistics do suggest that higher rates of insolvency occur in particular regions but it is very dangerous to generalize since, perhaps rather oddly, there are some localities within well performing areas which do badly on the insolvency front. It is not entirely clear why this should be and for this reason the data has not been included.

ARE THERE MORE INSOLVENCIES IN ANY PARTICULAR SECTOR?

The worst sector for insolvencies is the general category 'services' – with 46% of the total. Construction and manufacturing are second equal with 17% each. Retailing and wholesaling is third with 14% of insolvencies. The remaining 6% comprise all the 'other' sectors.

The services sector can be broken down, with business services represent-ing the highest proportion with 29% of the total of all insolvencies in a year, 10% for 'other' miscellaneous services, and 6% for leisure and tourism. The remaining 1% is for financial services.

Table A2.3   Analysis of insolvencies by sector in a typical year

Sector	Subsector	Percentage of all insolvencies p.a.
Services	Business services	29%
	Other misc. services	10%
	Leisure and tourism	6%
	Financial services	1%
Construction and transport		17%
Manufacturing		17%
Retailing and wholesale		14%
Other		6%
Total		100%

Source: Derived from data on the UK Government Insolvency Service website

What this table tells us is that perhaps the safest sector to work in, if you wish to minimize the prospects of insolvency, is financial services.

Retailing and wholesaling are often regarded as being high risks for insol-vency, but the data does not seem to support this view particularly, although it will vary according to whether the national economy is going through a boom or bust period, and to some extent on the degree of com-petition in a locality. There are also significant regional variations. In bad times the percentage of insolvencies in retailing and wholesaling can be as high as 20% of all insolvencies in a year, but in boom times can fall to around 14%. In general, wholesalers are twice as likely to become insolvent as retailers.

WHO ARE THE CREDITORS?

The creditors following an insolvency are shown in Figure A2.1. The two largest categories of creditors are the banks, with secured loans, etc., and unsecured creditors, e.g. suppliers. The next largest are 'other secured' creditors, with the remaining categories representing a very small percentage of the total.

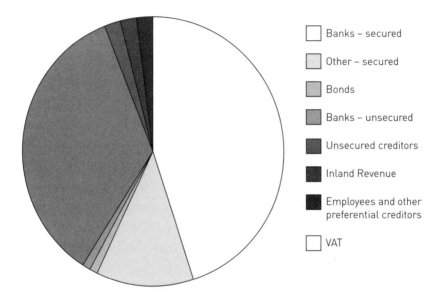

Figure A2.1   Creditor categories
Source: R3, the Association of Business Recovery Professionals 12th Corporate Insolvency Survey, see www.r3.org.uk

WHAT FORM OF LIQUIDATIONS OCCUR MOST IN A PARTICULAR SECTOR?

It is not unusual that when a smaller company goes into liquidation, the creditors seldom see much of their money. These creditors are often small companies themselves, who cannot themselves afford to have bad debts, and a domino effect of insolvencies can occur.

Interestingly the type of insolvency varies distinctly between industry sectors, as shown in Table A2.4.

Table A2.4 Most common insolvency procedure by sector

Sector	Most common insolvency procedure for sector
Retail and wholesale	Administration
Construction and transport	Compulsory or creditors voluntary liquidation
Manufacturing	Administration

Source: R3, the Association of Business Recovery Professionals 12th Corporate Insolvency Survey, see www.r3.org.uk

The data in this table, and other underlying data, suggests that in most sectors the concept of administration is becoming popular. This is because there is the hope of maximizing the returns for the creditors with this approach, and sometimes a hope of keeping at least some of the business intact.

Construction and transport has the highest percentage of compulsory liquidations, which comes about because the creditors feel forced to go to court to have a liquidator appointed, usually because the directors have not taken pre-emptive action. This happens either because they were blind to the problems, had inadequate accounting procedures and controls, or incurred some overwhelming expense (e.g. a tax or VAT bill).

HOW DO CREDITORS RECOVER MOST MONEY?

The data suggests that trade creditors are most likely to get more money back if they support a rescue of the failed company. As such, preferential creditors of a company which adopts a company voluntary arrangement (CVA) often receive three times as much money back compared with any other approach. At the other end of the spectrum a creditors' voluntary liquidation (CVL) does not usually generate the returns the creditors would ideally like, as can be seen in Figure A2.2.

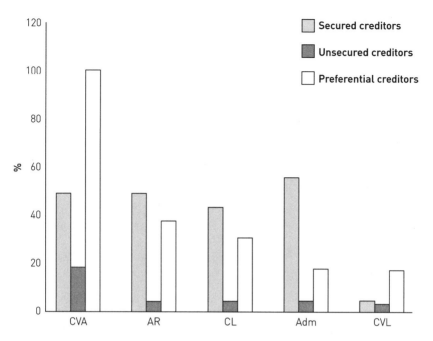

Note: CVA = company voluntary arrangement; AR = administrative receivership; CL = compulsory liquidation; Adm = administration; CVL = creditors voluntary liquidation

Figure A2.2 Percentage returns for creditors for different insolvency procedures

Source: R3, the Association of Business Recovery Professionals 12th Corporate Insolvency Survey, see www.r3.org.uk

JOB PRESERVATION FOLLOWING INSOLVENCY

Studies have suggested that across all sectors 41% of all jobs are preserved following an insolvency, however there are large variations between sectors as Figure A2.3 shows.

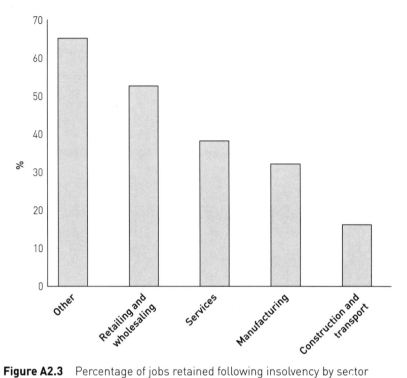

Figure A2.3 Percentage of jobs retained following insolvency by sector
Source: R3, the Association of Business Recovery Professionals 12th Corporate Insolvency Survey, see
www.r3.org.uk

Figure A2.4 shows the percentage of jobs retained by the insolvency
method used.

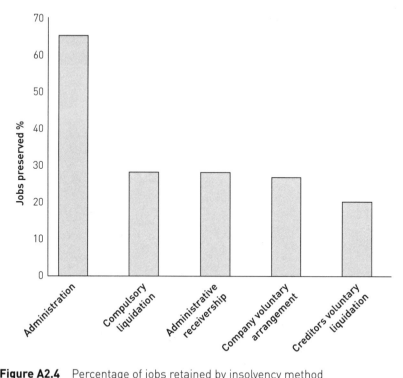

Figure A2.4   Percentage of jobs retained by insolvency method
Source: R3, the Association of Business Recovery Professionals 12th Corporate Insolvency Survey, see www.r3.org.uk

HOW MUCH DO COMPANIES TYPICALLY OWE WHEN THEY BECOME INSOLVENT?

On average companies owe some 140% of their annual turnover when they become insolvent, but this figure hides the fact that smaller businesses with turnovers of less than £1M p.a. which become insolvent typically owe significantly more than this.

(NB: the amount of debt companies have when they become insolvent also varies somewhat by region.)

OUTCOMES OF INSOLVENCY

The good news, and a credit to the insolvency practitioners, is that a break-up of the insolvent company's assets only occurs in 69% of cases. The other

31% are where the company survives either fully or partly, as shown in Figure A2.5.

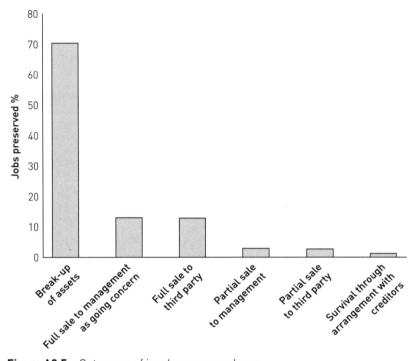

Figure A2.5 Outcomes of insolvency procedures
Source: R3, the Association of Business Recovery Professionals 12th Corporate Insolvency Survey, see www.r3.org.uk

Note that in 30% of cases the business continues in one form or another, either in full or in part, and owned either by the old management team, or by a third party.

Where a rescue is a possibility the rescue procedures, including administration, administrative receivership and company voluntary arrangement, can achieve excellent results, with a sale of either the whole or part of the company to either the management or a third party, as shown in Figure A2.6.

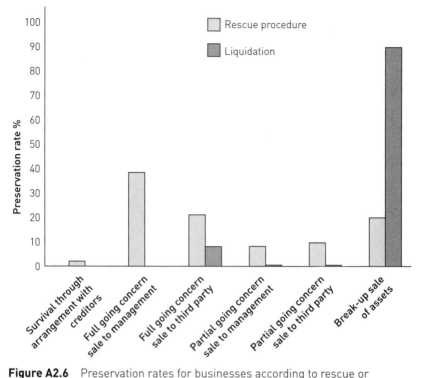

Figure A2.6   Preservation rates for businesses according to rescue or
liquidation approach

Source: R3, the Association of Business Recovery Professionals 12th Corporate Insolvency Survey, see
www.r3.org.uk

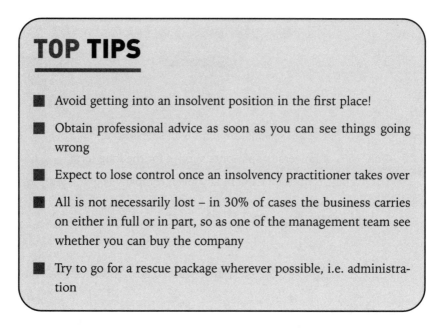

TOP TIPS

- Avoid getting into an insolvent position in the first place!

- Obtain professional advice as soon as you can see things going wrong

- Expect to lose control once an insolvency practitioner takes over

- All is not necessarily lost – in 30% of cases the business carries on either in full or in part, so as one of the management team see whether you can buy the company

- Try to go for a rescue package wherever possible, i.e. administration

Appendix 3
Fascinating business facts

- Only 30% of second generation family businesses survive
- Only 15% of university spin-outs survive for the long term
- The average term for a CEO in any given company is just 4 years
- 1 in 3 (33%) of start-ups fail within the first 3 years
- 1 in 4 (25%) of start-ups fail within 2 years
- 1 in 10 (10%) of start-ups fail within a year
- In a typical year in the UK some 450,000 new businesses are created
- There are 4.3M businesses in the UK comprising:
  - 2.0M sole traders
  - 1.8M registered companies
  - 0.5M partnerships
- Only 6,000 of the 4.3M businesses employ more than 250 staff
- 3.1M (of the 4.3M) businesses have no employees
- 23M people are employed in the private sector in the UK
- Almost 6M people are employed in the public sector in the UK
- Almost 5M people (20% of the private sector workforce) are thought to be employed by businesses funded by private equity (i.e. venture capital)
- 1.8M of the 4.3M businesses are registered for VAT
- There are twice as many men as women creating start-ups
- 50% of all innovations come from small companies
- 95% of radical innovations come from small companies
- Some 350,000 businesses cease trading in a typical year
- 20,000 companies are dissolved in the UK each year
- 35% of dissolved companies have been compulsorily liquidated
- 50% of dissolved companies have been voluntarily liquidated

▶ 15% of dissolved companies have been wound-up due to retirement, product not being needed any more, etc.

▶ Entrepreneurs have the potential to be successful in any sector

▶ Having a degree is not necessarily a guarantee of success

▶ 80% of businesses which are affected by a major disaster cease trading within 18 months of the disaster

▶ 40% of computer back-up procedures fail when restoration of data is attempted

Appendix 4
Glossary

This glossary is not an exhaustive list of business terms; it does however try to list those terms which businesspeople will come across from time to time and which appear in this book.

Administration order

Individuals: An order made in a court to arrange and administer the payment of debts by an individual

Companies: An order made by a court that appoints an administrator to take control of the company. A company can also be put into administration if a floating charge holder, or the directors of the company, file the requisite court notice.

Administrative receiver

An insolvency practitioner appointed by the holder of a debenture that is secured by a floating charge that covers the whole or substantially the whole of the company's assets. The insolvency practitioner's task is to realize those assets on behalf of the debenture holder.

Administrative receivership

The process whereby an insolvency practitioner is appointed by a debenture holder (lender) to realize the company's assets and pay preferential creditors and the debenture holder's debt. (Note: The right of a debenture holder to appoint an administrative receiver has been restricted by the Enterprise Act 2002 and administration is now generally the preferred course of action.)

Administrator

An insolvency practitioner appointed by the court under an administration order, by a floating charge holder, or by the company or its directors filing the requisite notice at court.

Board of directors

A body responsible to the shareholders for the running of a company.

Business
An industrial, commercial or professional services entity established to supply products and/or services to its customers.

Business angel
A high net wealth individual who wishes to invest in a start-up or fast-growing businesses.

CEO
Chief executive officer –usually the most senior executive director of the company and responsible to the board of directors for the running of the company.

Chairperson
The chairman/chairperson of the board of directors of a company, responsible primarily for chairing meetings of the board. The role is usually a non-executive one, but is in some companies an executive position.

Companies House
In the UK, the public sector entity reporting to the UK Government Department of Trade and Industry, which registers and holds relevant information (including annual reports and accounts) regarding all companies in the UK.

Company
A business enterprise registered with Companies House.

Compulsory liquidation
Winding-up of a company after a petition to the court, usually by a creditor.

COO
Chief operating officer – usually reports to the CEO and has responsibility for the day-to-day running of some or all of the company.

Creditor
An individual or business owed money by another individual or company.

Debt
Money owed to an individual or a company.

Debtor
An individual or company that owes money.

Debtor days
The number of days a payment is overdue.

Director
A person who is appointed to the board of directors of a company and who may have either an executive or a non-executive role.

Discounted cash flow (DCF)
This is a technique for assessing the attractiveness of an investment by discounting the free cash made available in each of the years of the project review, using the weighted average cost of capital, thereby arriving at a present value. If this is done for a number of projects you can compare the relative attractiveness of each, including the current cost of making the total investment upfront; it is a common technique for investment analysis.

Dividend
In a normal situation any payment distribution made to shareholders and paid out of profits. In an insolvency, any sum distributed to unsecured creditors.

Enterprise value
Enterprise value is the value attributed to a business (typically quoted companies), and is calculated by taking the market capitalization (i.e. share price × number of shares issued) plus all debt, less cash, and less any investments. It is a measure of the real value of a company as an enterprise rather than just pure market capitalization.

Fixed charge
A charge held over fixed assets. The debtor cannot sell the assets without the consent of the secured creditor or repaying the amount secured by the charge.

Floating charge
A charge held over the general assets of a company. The assets may change (e.g. stock) and the company can use the assets without the consent of the secured creditor until the charge becomes 'fixed'. It becomes fixed on the appointment of an administrative receiver, on the presentation of a winding-up petition or as otherwise provided for in the document creating the charge.

Guarantee

An agreement to pay a debt owed by a third party should the third party default on payment. It must be evidenced in writing for it to be enforceable.

HMRC

Her Majesty's Revenue and Customs, the government department in the UK responsible for collecting all taxes and customs revenues.

Limited liability company (ltd)

A company with limited liability.

Limited liability partnership (llp)

A partnership with limited liability.

Liquidation (or winding-up)

Liquidation applies to companies and partnerships. It involves the realization and distribution of the assets, and often the closing down of the business. There are three types of liquidation, namely compulsory, creditors' voluntary and members' voluntary liquidation.

Liquidator

The official receiver or an insolvency practitioner appointed to administer the liquidation of a company or partnership.

MBI

Management buy in – where external management buys some or all of the shares of a company so as to gain operating control.

MBO

Management buy out –where existing management buys some or all of the shares of its company and hence gains operating control of the company.

Member (of a company)

A person who has agreed to be, and is registered as, a member, such as a shareholder of a limited company.

Net present value (NPV)

NPV is the difference between the present value of cash in and the present value of cash out and is used in investment appraisal to help determine which projects are the most attractive financially.

NICs
National Insurance contributions.

Official receiver
An officer of the court and a civil servant employed by the Insolvency Service, which deals with bankruptcies and compulsory company liquidations.

Partner
A member of a partnership.

Partnership
A contractual relationship between two or more persons carrying on a joint business venture, each incurring liability for any losses, as well as the right to share in any profits.

Preferential creditor
A creditor who is entitled to receive certain payments in priority to floating charge holders and other secured creditors. These creditors include occupational pension schemes and employees.

Present value (PV)
What a sum of money at some time in the future is worth in today's money, assuming a given rate of return.

President
Not a role, or term, normally used in companies in the UK, although it is a common title in the USA where it can be synonymous with the title CEO. For some American companies operating internationally the head of a region is sometimes given the title of president. In smaller companies in the USA it is not uncommon to come across top executives with the combined roles/titles of chairman, president and CEO.

Public limited company (plc)
A company with limited liability whose shares may be sold to the public. There must be £50,000 of issued shares before the company can trade.

Receivership
A company in administrative receivership.

Secured creditor
A creditor who holds security, such as a mortgage, over a person's or company's assets for money owed.

Self-employed
Someone who works for themselves and is not employed by another person or company, and who is able to work for more than one customer.

Share(s)
A defined portion of the capital stock of a company.

Shareholder
The owner of one or more shares in a company.

SME
Small and medium sized enterprise.

Sole trader
A person working on their own account, who is self-employed, and is not registered as a company.

SWOT
Strengths, weaknesses, opportunities and threats relating to a company.

Unsecured creditor
A creditor who does not hold security (such as a mortgage) for money owed. An unsecured creditor may also be a preferential creditor.

VAT
Value added tax.

Venture capital
Capital investment in a company, which may be a high-risk investment, albeit with potentially significant gains if the valuation of the company increases rapidly following the investment.

Voluntary liquidation
A method of liquidation not involving the courts, or the official receiver. There are two types of voluntary liquidation – members' voluntary liquidation for solvent companies, and creditors' voluntary liquidation for insolvent companies.

Winding up order

An order of a court for the compulsory winding-up, or liquidation, of a company or partnership.

Appendix 5
Websites and further reading

USEFUL WEBSITES

Business advice and information

Institute of Directors	www.iod.com
Pensions advice	www.adviceonline.co.uk/pensions
Lawyers	www.infolaw.co.uk
Accountants	www.icaewfirms.co.uk
Venture capital	www.bvca.co.uk
Business angels	www.nban.co.uk
Federation of Small Businesses	www.fsb.org.uk
Business Link	www.businessquestionsanswered.co.uk
Chambers of commerce	www.britishchambers.org.uk
Federation of Enterprise Agencies	www.nfea.com
Startup co.	www.startupco.co.uk

Business angels

National Business Angel network	www.nban.co.uk
London Business Angels	www.lbangels.co.uk

Business Link

England	www.businesslink.gov.uk
Wales	www.businesseye.org.uk
Scotland	www.bgateway.com
Northern Ireland	www.investni.com
London	www.business4london.co.uk

Business magazines

Business XL/Growth Business   www.growthbusiness.co.uk
IoD Director   www.iod.com

Business mentors

British Volunteer Mentor
Programme   www.bvm.org.uk
The Prince's Trust   www.princes-trust.org.uk
Business Link   www.businesslink.gov.uk

Business statistics

Companies House   www.companieshouse.gov.uk
Small Business Service   www.sbs.gov.uk
Barclays Bank   www.barclaysbank.co.uk/business
Insolvency (R3, the Association of
Business Recovery Professionals)   www.r3.org.uk

Business websites

www.is4profit.com
www.businessgo.co.uk
www.smallbusiness.co.uk
www.newbusiness.co.uk

Commercial research

NOP   www.nop.co.uk
MORI   www.mori.com

Company information

Companies House   www.companieshouse.gov.uk
Company news and takeovers   www.ukbusinesspark.co.uk
Dun & Bradstreet   www.dbuk.dnb.com

Courts service

HM Courts Service   www.hmcourts-service.gov.uk

Design

Design Council   www.designdirectory.org
DTI best practice   www.dti.gov.uk/bestpractice

Enterprise agencies

National Federation of
Enterprise Agencies   www.nfea.com

Entrepreneurs community

www.gate2growth.com

Funding

DTI Collaborative Research &
Development   www.dti.gov.uk/crd
Knowledge Transfer Partnerships   www.ktponline.org.uk
Grants for businesses in assisted
areas   www.dti.gov.uk/regionalinvestment
R&D tax credits   www.dti.gov.uk/rd-guide/rd-taxcredit.htm

Grants for new ideas   www.dti.gov.uk/innovative-idea
Small Firms Loan Guarantee   www.dti.gov.uk/sflg
EU R&D grants   www.cordis.lu
Grants for science & technology   www.nesta.org.uk
Collaborative pre-commercial
research   www.ost.gov.uk/link
Faraday Partnerships   www.faradaypartnerships.org.uk
Grants for London businesses   www.london-innovation.org.uk
www.londonseedcapital.co.uk

	www.thecapitalfund.co.uk
	www.e-synergy.com
	www.bridgesventures.com
The Prince's Trust (for young people up to age 30)	www.princes-trust.org.uk

General sources of business information

Institute of Directors (free library and legal advice for members)	www.iod.com

Getting started

Business Link	www.businesslink.gov.uk/startup organiser

Government departments

Companies House	www.companieshouse.gov.uk
Inland Revenue (now HMRC)	www.hmrc.gov.uk
VAT	www.hmrc.gov.uk
DTI	www.dti.gov.uk
Department for Work and Pensions	www.dwp.gov.uk
Insolvency service	www.insolvency.gov.uk
Patent Office	www.patent.gov.uk
Small Business Service	www.sbs.gov.uk

Grant information

J4B grant finder service	www.j4b.co.uk
Business Link	www.businesslink.co.uk
Small Business Service	www.sbs.gov.uk

Human resources

Institute of Directors (free HR and legal advice for members)	www.iod.com

CIPD (professional HR body
for UK)   www.cipd.co.uk
Viking Direct (supplies pro
forma HR manual)   www.viking.co.uk

Insolvency

Association of Insolvency
Professionals   www.r3.org.uk
Insolvency service   www.insolvency.gov.uk

Knowledge transfer

Academia   www.ktponline.org.uk
Government   www.dti.gov.uk/ktn

Manufacturing websites

Manufacturing Advisory Service   www.mas.co.uk
London Manufacturing Advisory
Service   www.mas-london.co.uk
Centre for Manufacturing
Excellence   www.ceme.co.uk

Market information

UK Trade & Investment   www.uktradeinvest.gov.uk
Trade Association Forum   www.taforum.org
Office for National Statistics   www.statistics.gov.uk
European Information Centres   www.euro-info.org.uk

Market research

British Market Research Assoc.   www.bmra.org.uk
Research Buyers' Guide   www.rbg.org.uk
International research   www.esomar.org
organizations   www.worldopinion.com

New media

New Media Knowledge   www.nmk.co.uk

Patents

UK Patent Office   www.ukpats.org.uk
British Library patents collection www.bl.uk/patents
DTI innovation promotion   www.innovation.gov.uk
Trevor Bayliss Foundation   www.thetbf.org

Red tape

Better regulation executive www.betterregulation.gov.uk
S/W to help comply with legal
regulations   www.policymatter.com

Regional support

Help for disadvantaged
communities in London   www.one-london.com

Sales and marketing advice

Marketing Information Portal www.marketinguk.co.uk
Institute of Marketing   www.cim.co.uk
Direct Marketing Association www.dma.org.uk

Start-up organizer

Business Link   www.businesslink.gov.uk/startup
             organiser

Support groups

Chambers of commerce   www.britishchambers.org.uk

Technology transfer

www.london-irc.org

Trade associations

www.taforum.org

Venture capital

British Venture Capital Assoc.	www.bvca.co.uk
Corporate Venturing	www.corporateventuringuk.org
Downstream funding	www.singlepathway.com

FURTHER READING

Accounting

FT Guide to Using and Interpreting Company Accounts
Wendy McKenzie
Financial Times Prentice Hall

Magic Numbers
Peter Temple
John Wiley & Sons

Accounting for Non-accountants
Graham Mott
Kogan Page

Accounts Demystified
Antony Rice
Prentice Hall

Business plans

The Definitive Business Plan
Richard Stutely
Financial Times Prentice Hall

The Business Plan Workbook
Colin Barrow et al.
The Sunday Times Business Enterprise Series
Kogan Page

Business start-up	*FT Guide to Business Start Up* Sara Williams Financial Times Prentice Hall
Company secretary	*The Company Secretary's Handbook* Helen Ashton The Sunday Times Business Enterprise Series Kogan Page
Director's handbook	*The Director's Handbook* Pinsent Masons IoD/Kogan Page
Employment law	*The Employer's Handbook* Barry Cushway IoD/ Kogan Page
Entrepreneurship	*Mastering Entrepreneurship* Sue Birley and Daniel Muzyka Financial Times Prentice Hall *The High-Tech Entrepreneur's Handbook* Jack Lang Financial Times Prentice Hall
Government rules and regulations	*The No-nonsense guide to Government Rules and Regulations for Setting up your Business* Business Link
Growing businesses	*The Growing Business Handbook* Adam Jolly (ed.) IoD/Kogan Page
Health and safety	*The Health and Safety Handbook* Jeremy Stranks IoD/Kogan Page
Marketing plan	*The Highly Effective Marketing Plan* Peter Knight Prentice Hall Business

Outsourcing

The Outsourcing Handbook
Mark J Power et al.
Kogan Page

Pricing

Smarter Pricing
Tony Cram
Financial Times Prentice Hall

Raising finance

Raising Finance
Paul Barrow
The Sunday Times Business Enterprise Series
Kogan Page

Sales and selling

Selling and Sales Management
David Jobber and Geoff Lancaster
Financial Times Prentice Hall

Selling a business

The Complete Guide to Selling your Business
Paul S. Sperry and Beatrice H. Mitchell
The Sunday Times Business Enterprise Series
Kogan Page

Index